STEVE COLLINS

Twice a world champion, at middleweight and super-middleweight, Collins is currently at the top in his sport. In Millstreet in March 1995 he faced his greatest challenge, Chris Eubank. In this book he gives a fascinating insight into the physical and mental preparations for his fights. He also tells of the years of slog and the difficulty of making it in the toughest profession of all – boxing.

A UNIQUE BEHIND-THE-SCENES
ACCOUNT OF THE BOXING WORLD AT
TOP INTERNATIONAL LEVEL

PAUL HOWARD

Aged twenty-four, Paul works as a freelance journalist in Dublin. He trained as a news reporter with *Southside*, then spent two years with the *Dublin Tribune*. Covering Steve Collins fights, he travelled to New Jersey, Italy, London, Belfast, Sheffield, Hong Kong, Boston and Millstreet, reporting for a number of Irish and British newspapers. He has written extensively about sport for the *Sunday Tribune*, and his work has also appeared in the *Sunday Times* and the *Irish Times*.

CELTIC WARRIOR

STEVE COLLINS
with Paul Howard

THE O'BRIEN PRESS
DUBLIN

First published 1995 by The O'Brien Press Ltd.,
20 Victoria Road, Rathgar, Dublin 6, Ireland.

British Library Cataloguing-in-publication Data
A catalogue reference for this book is available from the British Library.

ISBN 0-86278-439-5

2 4 6 8 10 9 7 5 3 1
96 98 00 02 04 03 01 99 97 95

Typesetting, layout, editing, design: The O'Brien Press Ltd.
Cover photo: INPHO/Billy Stickland
Printing: ColourBooks Ltd., Dublin

Acknowledgements

I would like to thank my wife, Gemma, for her patience and support throughout my boxing career and my three children, Caoimhe, Stevie and Clodagh, for giving me great joy. Also my late father, Paschal, and my mother, Colette, for happiness and security throughout my wonderful childhood.

To all my family, close friends and loyal supporters I offer my sincere thanks.

I also thank my trainer Freddy King, my sparring partners, gym companions, and Tony Quinn for sharing his wisdom with me. Thank you.

Last but not least I want to thank God.

STEVE COLLINS

Acknowledgements

An enormous debt of gratitude is owed to my mother and father whose interest in my writing continues to be my greatest motivation. Thanks are also owed to Gerry Murtagh and Martin Walsh for encouraging me to pursue my ambitions in journalism, and to Ken Finlay, Brendan Fanning and Ger Siggins for helping me to realise them. The warmth and hospitality shown to me by the Collins family – particularly Gemma, Colette, Roddy, Mick and Paschal during the months I worked on this book and the years I've spent covering Steve's career will never be forgotten. Neither will the assistance given to me by the Egan family. A very special word of thanks is due to the Sunday Tribune's Dave Hannigan, who not only edited the early manuscripts, but offered encouragement, advice, inspiration and humour whenever necessary. And lastly, I'd like to thank Steve Collins, who is in every sense the greatest fighter I've ever known.

PAUL HOWARD

Contents

PROLOGUE

I sat down on the stool for the last time and filled my lungs with air, unaware that, across the ring, Ronnie Davies was slapping Chris Eubank in the face and shouting: 'If you don't knock him out or stop him, you've lost the fight.'

The pace had taken its toll on the two of us. We were both pushing back the bounds of exhaustion as we walked towards the middle of the ring for the last time. After thirty-three minutes, we understood each other so intimately that we were probably alone in knowing that there wasn't going to be a knockdown. The referee stood between us, keeping us apart with his outstretched arms and he ordered us to touch gloves. The ritual over, Eubank charged straight for me in one last desperate throw.

A barrage of wild shots missed me on the ropes and I walked away. His mouth was open and he was panting. The noise in the arena was intense and hearing the chants of 'STEEEVE-OOOHH' gave me the impetus to dig deep for the strength to stand toe-to-toe with him for the first time in the fight. We both let go with everything we had. I smiled at Eubank and he nodded at me, as though he respected me for withstanding what he'd just thrown. I continued on, driving, driving, driving. Much of his work now had the mark of a desperate man about it, and he accidentally caught me with his head coming inside. He took the full brunt of it himself, stumbling back against the ropes and I punched him as he tried to tie my arms up. We exchanged body punches. With about a minute to go, I caught him with a solid right and he seemed to me to waver a bit. I looked down at his legs and they had buckled. Had it happened in the early part of the fight, I'd have finished him off. His hands were aloft again and he tried to taunt me. I stepped backwards and he charged at me, until we fell back against the ropes, then, as he went to draw a punch I pawed at him and slipped away, and he fell against the ropes and was left looking out into the crowd. Our arms punch-weary, almost to the point of limpness, we stood off each other for a few seconds. Eubank performed one last dance and beckoned me forward again. I threw an aimless shot in his direction and we fell into a clinch. The bell sounded.

My brother, Roddy, who has a remarkable talent for breaching security cordons and getting into boxing rings, already stood in front of me by the time I turned around to walk back to my corner. His two forefingers in the air in front of him, he looked at me and shouted: 'Means to an end, Stephen. Means to an end.'

It wasn't until a few days later that I realised what he meant.

CHAPTER I

Starting Over

HOME SWEET HOME-FROM-HOME

Take the London Underground from Liverpool Street to Romford in Essex, turn left when you leave the station, and head up the town. Just past a cluster of fast-food restaurants – McDonald's, Kentucky Fried Chicken and Pizza Hut – take a right turn. Fifty yards up the road there's a large, whitewashed building with a plate-glass front that somehow seems ill at ease among the shopfronts and grey houses on Romford High Street. It could be any number of things – a council rent office, a building society, a dental surgery. But this is Matchroom Headquarters and the building is a temple, built in honour of Barry Hearn, the smooth-talking son of a Dagenham bus driver who has become Britain's leading sports promoter and a self-made millionaire. On any given day, Hearn spends eight or nine hours sitting in his office upstairs, arguing, persuading, berating, cajoling, pleading, browbeating and charming people into doing business his way.

Downstairs, the expensively-carpeted offices are alive with the loud chattering of his staff. Sharing Hearn's charm, enthusiasm and insatiable appetite for work appears to be a prerequisite for getting a job at Matchroom. When you step into the office on a winter's day, the warmth and cosiness of the place hits you immediately. People use your name when they greet you and sound genuinely interested when they ask: 'Aw roight, Steve, 'ow's it goin'?'

Next door, hiding at the side, is a grim-looking detached house that you wouldn't expect to stand so close to such a beautiful building. You push the door, go through the porch and the first sight that greets you is five or maybe ten thousand programmes left over from the Chris Eubank/Nigel Benn fight in 1992, stacked from floor to ceiling in twenty or thirty damp piles. Beside them is a payphone, which was in perfect working order until some highly-strung boxer worked himself up into a rage when he couldn't get through to his girlfriend and put his fist through the numbers panel on the front. It is still possible to phone an outside number, provided it doesn't contain 3, 6 or 9. Mine does, so my wife phones me instead. My nightly calls from Gemma are the only contact I have with my family while I'm here, but the draught in the hallway and the stench from the mildewed programmes would discourage you from spending too much time talking.

At the front of the house there's a living room, where you can watch television if you can somehow balance the aerial on the headrest of the sofa, which seems to be the only point in the room where you can pick up a clear signal. Upstairs, there's a communal kitchen, where you'll find week-old copies of *The Sun* strewn around the floor, used teabags in the sink and half a can of beans a couple of months past its sell-by date in the fridge. Downstairs again, through the second door on the right, is my bedroom. A spartan room with a bed, a wardrobe, a clothes horse, a portable television and a two-bar electric heater, which keeps the room just about warm enough to bear.

This is home during the week. When training finishes every Friday afternoon, I pick up my bags, take a taxi through the early-evening rush-hour traffic to Stansted airport and catch a flight back to Dublin, where Gemma will be waiting with the children. On Sunday, I'm saying goodbye to them again for another week, and my children, Caoimhe and Stevie, have come to know Romford as Daddy's house.

I have another name for it. When journalists from Dublin phone for the latest update on how my training is going and for news on an upcoming fight, I always refer to it sardonically as 'The Romford Villa'.

It was quite amusing to discover later that for almost a year journalists in Dublin had been saying things like: 'Steve Collins has been training at the luxurious Romford Villa', painting very colourful images of a plush, Gran Canaria-style apartment complex with jacuzzis, steamrooms and a swimming pool!

I could afford greater comfort than this. A room in a local hotel or guesthouse would not be beyond my means, especially since my expenses are tax deductible. That wouldn't do me any good. Sacrifice and austerity – they're the laws that govern a boxer's life. They're in everything we do. Boxing isn't a job, it's a vocation. The successful ones will live like monks. We don't work a nine-to-five day. We work all of the time. I'm working when I'm craving a bacon sandwich in the middle of the evening, but can't have one because I know I'll have to work twice as hard in the gym the following day to sweat the weight off. I'm working when I'm explaining to my friends that I can't go out for a drink with them because I have to be up early the following morning for roadwork. I'm working when I'm resisting the temptation to knock off the alarm clock, roll over in the bed and fall asleep again when it's time to pull on my tracksuit and get out onto the roads. I'm hungry all the time. What I eat in a day when I'm in training I'd eat during one meal when I'm off. At night I'm exhausted and I'm sore. I miss my wife's company and I miss my children so much that I can't talk to them on the phone every night because it upsets me too much.

These are the things that make the difference between a champion and a run-of-the-mill boxer. Champions have to stay hungry and angry. The analogy most often used is the one about the two puppies who are taken from the same litter. One grows up in a big house and spends its day sitting by the fireside and being fed cake. The other grows up in a working-class housing estate and spends its day chasing cars, scavenging through litter bins and being kicked in the arse. It's the dog who hasn't been pampered who'll survive if they're both thrown out onto the streets. It's no coincidence that boxers are drawn almost exclusively from tough, working-class backgrounds or that world champions who've taken to extravagant living once they've reached millionaire status don't usually keep their title belts for long.

It's this thought that gets me through the early-morning roadwork and my day in the gym, a hundred yards down the road. The 6am alarm call is a sound I've never got used to. But I throw back the covers as soon as it goes off, so I know, while I'm staring at the ceiling, wishing in my state of semi-consciousness that this wasn't happening, that I can't go back to sleep again. My next opponent might be out there somewhere pounding the roads already. Maybe he's been up half an hour. Or an hour. And I know I have to be hungrier than he is.

IMPETUS FOR A NEW START IN 1994

I'm not George Foreman. I have absolutely no intention of fighting until I'm forty-six or forty-seven. Approaching my thirtieth birthday, I knew that I had, at best, three or four years left on the clock. But 1993 had been the most frustrating year of my life. I'd spent about half of it away from my family and had earned hardly any money, while boxers who hadn't as much talent, I felt, had become world champions and were earning millions by defending their titles against weak opponents. After seven and a half years as a professional boxer, I was back to square one again. My past counted for nothing. The world title fights against Mike McCallum and Reggie Johnson, my Irish title, my US title, my fights against Sumbu Kalambay, Tony Thornton and Kevin Watts, nobody cared about who I'd fought, what I'd won or who I'd known. I was an undercard fighter again at the start of 1994, boxing to kill time on somebody else's big night, while the television stations were getting ready to go live with the main event; boxing against second-rate opponents in front of a couple of hundred disinterested people who couldn't wait until the fight was over so they could see 'the real action'.

I felt a bit like one of those footballers who, after a long and distinguished career with a club like Manchester United or Liverpool, suddenly finds himself, in his early thirties, transferred to a club like Doncaster or Rotherham, but who never stops dreaming about returning to Old

Trafford or Anfield for an FA Cup match to score the winning goal and knock his old club out.

Throughout my career, despite all the disappointments, I never stopped believing, like that footballer, that there were better days ahead. I never stopped believing that I would be a world champion. Every New Year's Eve, I'd tell Gemma the same thing: 'This is going to be my year.' Every New Year's Eve since 1986. But this year, I'd decided, would be the last time I'd ever say it. Because if I didn't win a world title in 1994, I was quitting boxing for good. What I'd do for money, I didn't know. Perhaps I'd dig out my toolbag and go back to being an electrician. Or I might end up on the dole. Whatever I did, I wasn't boxing any more, because I couldn't take many more years like 1993.

After Christmas, though, I returned to Romford with a little more enthusiasm than I when I had left, because I knew that, as well as the world title shot that I'd been told was only a matter of months away, I also had something more tangible on which to focus. Gemma and I had found a plot of land in Castleknock, close to the house we were renting, which we thought would be an ideal site on which to build our dream home. It was about an acre and a half in size, with stables set to one side. As a child, I used to spend my summers working in the stables in the Castleknock area and have had an abiding fascination with horses ever since. I'd always promised my own children that if I ever became rich, we'd buy a farm and I'd get them ponies. When a neighbour told me that the land was about to be put up for sale, I became very excited about it and, after making a few discreet inquiries, discovered that it belonged to Ben Dunne, the multi-millionaire supermarket tycoon. His house was directly in front of the one we were living in at the time. I'd never met him before, but knew his reputation as a very tough businessman and wondered whether I'd be up to the job of negotiating with him.

Getting to meet him, as it happened, was a difficult task in itself. I finally managed to get a telephone number, phoned it, left a message and waited by the phone for Ben Dunne to call. In the meantime, though, anxious to get a straight Yes or No before I headed back to Romford, I made other efforts to try to get a message to him. A friend of mine knew a friend of his and, after various third-hand messages were relayed back and forth, he invited me across to his house to discuss it. I was nervous as I walked up Ben Dunne's driveway that day. It was a new feeling for me. Facing some of the most fearsome fighters in the middleweight division hadn't frightened me. Negotiating with the toughest promoters in the toughest business of all had not intimidated me. I'd had dinner with famous television personalities, sports stars and city mayors and had never felt as nervous as this. This was new, because Ben Dunne had something that I wanted dearly and I knew he was so wealthy that it didn't really matter to him whether I offered him a million pounds or twenty pounds for the land. After he met me at the door with a handshake, I put all of my cards on the table: 'Ben, I want you to know I've fought for world titles in the most intimidating atmospheres you could imagine and I've sat down with sharks and made deals that would shape my future. But I'm more nervous meeting you than I've ever been in my whole life. Not because of who you are, but because you have something that I want and I'm standing here with you, not knowing whether I'm going to get it or not.'

It was the perfect ice-breaker. More accustomed to doing business with people who never let on just how much deals meant to them, he seemed to appreciate my honesty. We hit it off immediately, talked about boxing, about sport, about Dublin. I was struck by how down-to-earth he was. Eventually, he stood up and said: 'Come on, we'll go take a look at the land.' We got into his car and drove the short distance to the top of a crooked country road, got out and walked across the land. He'd already decided to sell it to me and setting the price seemed to be just a formality we'd tie up later. We signed nothing, but made a gentleman's agreement with a handshake. Now I had the incentive I needed to return to Romford to start training. The money from my next four or five fights would be used to build a house on the land and Gemma and I started drawing plans in our minds. Ben Dunne had impressed me. He was only the second person I'd ever done business with who was prepared to take me at face value. The first was Barry Hearn.

Hearn had been my manager for over a year and had never asked me to put my name to a piece of paper to prove it. We first spoke shortly before Christmas in 1992, a few weeks after I had lost a European title fight to Sumbu Kalambay in Italy, though I still believe I should have been the winner. Utterly disillusioned with boxing, I wasn't sure whether I ever wanted to get into a ring again. My eighteen-month contract with my manager Barney Eastwood was up. A few managers had phoned to make me offers, but none of them said anything that would convince me to continue fighting. Until I spoke to Hearn. The others talked percentages, contracts, clauses and options. He talked boxing. He was a great communicator. I sat on the stairs of the house we lived in on the Navan Road with the phone to my ear, listening as he told me that he was going to help me resurrect my career. As well as the frustration of losing to Kalambay, my previous world title defeats to Mike McCallum and Reggie Johnson still rankled with me. Hearn told me they didn't matter. He was going to get me another world title fight.

By the end of 1993, he'd brought me most of the way there. The previous June in London, I'd stopped a very durable South African called Gerhard Botes in seven rounds to win the vacant World Boxing Organisation (WBO) Penta-Continental middleweight title. It was only a junior world title, but winning it helped make me the number one contender for the WBO middleweight title. The champion was Chris Pyatt, who had won the belt by outpointing my old enemy Kalambay a month earlier. I felt I had actually beaten Kalambay more convincingly in my fight even if the judges didn't agree with me. But Pyatt had fought him in Leicester and not in Kalambay's adopted country, Italy. After twelve rounds, he got the same decision I felt I should have got two years earlier and now he was a world champion. Since I'd become the number one contender, the rules said that he had six months in which to agree terms for a fight against me.

Because we were the same age and fought at the same weight, I had always taken an interest in Pyatt's career and knew quite a bit about him. As a teenager, he was one of Britain's most precocious amateurs and a queue of promoters was waiting for his signature when he returned from the Commonwealth Games with a gold medal in 1983. As a professional, his reputation was as a knockout specialist, with thirty of his forty-two victories coming inside the distance, and he had previously held the British, European and Commonwealth titles at light middleweight. Only three men had beaten him as a pro and two of them, Gianfranco Rosi and John David Jackson, were still world champions. After spending four years with promoter Frank Warren, he had joined Matchroom in 1992, after sparring an exhibition bout with Chris Eubank at the Michael Watson benefit dinner in London. He impressed Eubank, who took him on as his full-time sparring partner. It revitalised Pyatt's career and, shorn of the dreadlocks that had made him so distinguishable, he beat the Colombian Adolpho Caballero, to win the vacant World Boxing Council (WBC) international middleweight title. Like me, he'd arrived at a half-way house on the road to a world title. He finally got his shot seven months later, when Gerald McClellan relinquished the title and Pyatt was nominated to fight Kalambay for it.

Pyatt had already made his first defence in September 1993, knocking out a former Eubank opponent, the Argentinian Hugo Corti, in six rounds. I was next in line. Or so I thought. I'd waited for Hearn to make some kind of announcement that autumn. October passed. November passed. And still nothing. Every day, people were asking me when it was going to happen and all I could tell them was that I still hadn't been told anything. All Hearn would say was that it was in the pipeline. Into December and still no news. Then, back in Dublin one weekend before Christmas, I received a very disturbing phonecall from a friend in England. ''Ave you 'eard about Pyatt, Steve?' he asked.

'No, what about him?'

'Well, he's not fighting you next at all. It's just been announced. He's fighting that South African bloke, Mark Cameron, on February the twenty-fourth.'

I thought he was joking but I heard the fight announced on television that night. I went berserk. The only thing that had kept me enthusiastic about fighting during the previous twelve months was the thought that I was at least making some progress towards a world title fight. And nobody had even bothered to phone me to tell me that Pyatt was fighting someone else. I thought it best not to ring Hearn until I'd calmed down. When I did, he explained that ITV weren't that interested in a Pyatt/Collins fight and weren't offering him much money to televise it. Also, Pyatt knew he was putting his title very much on the line by fighting me and he wanted one more payday to make some money in case I beat him. My fight with Pyatt would still go ahead, Hearn assured me. I had no other choice but reluctantly to accept it. I told Hearn I wanted a warm-up fight too. The only fight I'd had since the summer was against the Welsh champion, Wayne Ellis, whom I'd stopped in nine rounds. Hanging around until April or May 1994 or whenever Pyatt decided to fight me could leave me out of condition and fight-practice. Hearn said he'd get me an opponent, and he phoned me back a couple of days later to say he'd pencilled my name onto the undercard of the same show, which would take place at Brentwood on 9 February, and not 24 February as originally planned. My opponent hadn't been named yet, but I knew he wouldn't be world class, so I was unlikely to earn much money from it.

POLITICAL PRISONER

Boxing had helped me develop an instinctive distrust of people. My faith in Barry Hearn had been rocked and I could no longer be sure of anything. The deal with Ben Dunne had managed to give me something of a lift over Christmas, but the enthusiasm with which I returned to Romford in January '94 lasted no more than a couple of days and I began to feel depressed. The weekdays in the gym seemed to be lengthening, the weekends at home shortening and I seemed to be getting no closer to a world title fight. As the winter wore on, there were nights when I lay awake wondering whether, as hard as I was working in the gym at the end of Romford High Street each day, someone wasn't working just as hard in the office a hundred yards away to ensure that I never climbed into the same ring as Pyatt. It wasn't inconceivable. Hearn promoted and managed both of us and there seemed to be little advantage for him in staging a fight just to see a world title change hands from one of his fighters to another. If I could be convinced to set my sights on one of the other three world titles instead, then he might well end up with two world middleweight champions to promote rather than one.

The concept of having four 'world champions' at each weight will confuse those not entirely familiar with the politics of boxing. The reason behind it becomes clearer once you start to appreciate the power and influence that promoters enjoy and why, quite often, fights take place only on their say-so. In most other sports, there's no room for ambiguity: the governing body stages a world championship tournament with the best snooker players, swimmers, athletes or whatever going to a certain country to compete, and the winners are deemed to be 'world champions'. Boxing, though, has four self-appointed governing bodies – the World Boxing Association (WBA), the World Boxing Council (WBC), the International Boxing Federation (IBF) and the World Boxing Organisation (WBO) – each of which offers its own world titles and each of which is heavily dependent on money from promoters to exist. Their sanctioning fee for a bout can be as much as three percent of a promotion's gross takings. With the backing of one of the four, the promoter/manager can then approach a television company and sell the fight as a 'world title' bout.

But it's very important to remember that, while the 'governing' bodies compile lists of rankings for boxers and nominate contenders for world titles, they are being bankrolled by a handful of promoters and managers. So, in boxing, we have arrived at this ludicrous situation where the 'police' depend on the people they're supposed to be policing. Which is, of course, the source of all the allegations of corruption in boxing. If a promoter or manager is unhappy with the treatment he's getting for one of his fighters from one governing body, he'll simply take his business and his three-percent sanctioning fee to another one. It's why you sometimes hear about managers getting their fighters high rankings, world title fights and favourable judging decisions against the odds. While I'm not trying to evoke Machiavellian images here of corrupt officials sitting down with promoters to sell ratings and world title shots, they have discovered what I'll describe as the mutual benefit in a harmonious co-existence.

Since the summer of 1993, I'd been the official number one contender for Pyatt's title. But because he controlled both of us, Hearn could have asked the WBO to grant Pyatt an extension to the deadline by which he had to agree to fight me. An extension of three months, for instance, might have left me so dispirited and so hard-up for money that I'd have been convinced to fight for one of the other world titles instead. Most sportsmen aren't required to understand the politics of their sport. For boxers, it's an imperative.

WITHOUT DIRECTION

I struggled through January in the gym, convinced that there was a conspiracy to keep Pyatt and myself apart. I felt completely alone in Romford. One afternoon in particular stands out. As I packed my gearbag for the gym, I was told that Hearn wanted to talk to me next door. The talk, as I remember it, was a general one about how I was progressing in the gym and a reassurance that he had big plans for me. As he spoke, my eyes were panning the walls of his office, looking at the framed photographs of all the fighters he was involved with – Chris Eubank, Nigel Benn, Herbie Hide, Francis Ampufo. There was none of me. I hadn't done anything to make him proud of me. But taking pride of place on the wall behind his desk was a large photograph of him embracing Chris Pyatt on the night Pyatt beat Kalambay. It was so warm, the kind of hug a father gives a son. How I got through training that afternoon, I don't know. That night, I was at my lowest ebb. The photograph ... this symbol of Hearn's paternal love for the man he said he wanted me to fight ... I couldn't get it out of my mind. I kept thinking: Shit, Steve, how are you going to break that up?

I was very jealous. Pyatt's record was nowhere near as impressive as mine, yet he had a world title buckled around his waist. I believed I wasn't going to get a shot at it and I would have to grovel for something that I felt I'd earned. On 9 February, Pyatt would be fighting someone who would earn more money than me. I hated the thought of having to fight on Pyatt's undercard and I hated the fact that I was getting mug's money to do it.

By the middle of January, I was convinced that Hearn had plans to manoeuvre me in another direction. Then he spoke to me one morning about a possible fight in the United States against Vinnie Pazienza, a thirty-one-year-old former world champion who had made an extraordinary comeback to the ring after breaking his neck in a car crash. Hearn knew Pazienza's life story and was very excited about matching me with him. Newspaper photographs of him putting himself through gruelling weight sessions while wearing a neck brace had turned him into something of a small-time American hero late in his career, while his flamboyant style, complete with fringed trunks, tasseled boots and a psyching-up routine that involved punching himself on the chin while leading the crowd in a chant of 'Yeah, Yeah, Yeah,' had made him an enormous box-office attraction and a favourite with the television networks. He was squat, strong and muscular, didn't possess a knockout punch, but had what the Americans call 'a chin-first style' that had taken him through dozens of all-out wars in the ring. Since making what doctors had described as an impossible comeback, he'd had six straight victories, including a win over former world welterweight champion Lloyd Honeyghan, which had caught the fight-public's attention in Britain. A match with him could be very lucrative, Hearn suggested. His popularity in the US had pushed him up into the million-dollar-per-fight bracket. But he held no title. Despite Hearn's effusiveness, beating Pazienza would do little or nothing to bolster my claim for a third world title shot. No, for me it was Pyatt or nobody at all.

Being champion of the world was something I'd had as an ambition since I started boxing. By January 1994, I had come to realise that it was an obsession, one that was eating away at me like a neurosis. It was on my mind when I woke in the morning and still there when I went to sleep at night. There were nights when I lay awake, asking myself what the hell I was doing, when I seriously considered walking out of my life in the squalid little house in Romford and in the sweatshop down the road where I was spending afternoons deluding myself that I could be middleweight champion of the world.

Barry Hearn, I thought, was stalling because he didn't want me to fight Chris Pyatt. And if my manager didn't want me to fight him, there was no way I was going to. I knew I was good enough to beat Pyatt, but that didn't count for anything. I thought about going back to America, considered pursuing some of the offers I'd been made by other managers. But more often, I just thought about packing it in and catching the earliest flight out of Stansted to go back to Gemma and the children and start to be a proper husband and a normal father to them. I missed Gemma so much, missed her company. This was never her dream. It was always mine. But for eight years she'd been willing to live it, had turned her life upside-down for it, and had never once complained. Had I stayed on at Guinness's all those years ago, I could have been a senior engineer, we could have bought a nice house on my salary, taken a holiday once a year and reared our family together. I wouldn't have had to spend all of my time away from her, living in a kip in Essex with a bunch of men who don't know how to tidy up after themselves. Back in Dublin, she was heavily pregnant and, as usual, having to cope on her own.

Upset, disillusioned and more confused about my future than at any stage in my life, I flew back to Ireland one weekend towards the end of January, determined to erase any thoughts about boxing from my mind for the two days I was going to spend in Dublin. Gemma and the children were waiting in the Arrivals lounge at Dublin Airport and I thought I was going to cry as Stevie and Caoimhe came charging towards me and jumped up into my arms. It felt so good to see Gemma again. All the frustration and unhappiness that had been pent up inside me for weeks poured out as we drove back to the house we were renting on the Navan Road and Gemma listened, sympathetic as always. I was looking forward to getting back to the things I'd missed. Hugs, words of encouragement, Caoimhe showing me the latest steps she'd learned at Irish dancing, Stevie telling me about his day at school. A quiet Friday night in front of the television with Gemma was what appealed to me most. And food. A week in England, living on a strict diet of porridge for breakfast, meat and vegetables for dinner and bread and butter for tea, had left me famished. I had just started to tuck into a big meal when the telephone rang. It was my trainer, Freddy King.

'We've got a fight for you if you're interested, mate,' he told me. But the big news was that it was on the following night!

'Oh go on, Steve, we're a bit stuck,' Freddy cajoled. 'It's against Johnny Melfah, up in Belfast. His opponent's gone and pulled out.'

I was over my fighting weight as it was – even before the meal – and taking a fight at twenty-four hours' notice would give me no time at all to prepare. Also, I need to condition myself psychologically, as much as physically, to build up feelings about an opponent, feelings of resentment or hatred or whatever. That's why I train away from home. Because you can't ask a boxer to be a family man one day and then suddenly to be a fighter the next. The two are incompatible. But that's what I was being asked to do.

The weight excuse wouldn't wash, because the fight was at super-middleweight, 12 stone 2lbs, which I could just about make. And it wasn't as if I knew nothing about the opponent they were offering me. I'd beaten Melfah before, stopping him in three rounds just a year earlier in my first fight under Hearn. Back then, he'd lost ten out of twenty-three fights, but he had once been in with Britain's best, including Herol Graham, Chris Eubank and Nicky Piper. The last time we fought, he cut me with his head. It was a small nick just above my forehead, but those kind of cuts tend to bleed a lot and, had I not finished him off a few minutes later, the cut might have opened up just enough to convince the referee to stop it. Back then, I was piecing my career together again and had nothing to lose. This time, I was the number one contender for a world title. What if he caught me with his head going into a clinch? If I lost on a cut, my career would be as good as over. But Matchroom were badly stuck. Melfah had been scheduled to fight Sammy Storey from Belfast on the undercard of Eamonn Loughran's title fight against Alessandro Duran at the King's Hall. But Storey withdrew through injury, leaving Hearn without another 'name' on the bill. Fight fans in Belfast would feel seriously shortchanged unless an Irish fighter could be found to replace Storey.

'Well, how much money's in it?' I asked.

'Ballpark ... two thousand pounds.'

I felt I should get more than that; after all, I was putting everything on the line. But finally I agreed to do it – after all, they were stuck.

MELFAH IN BELFAST

Our plans for a quiet night home in front of the 'Late Late Show' in ruins, I threw some clothes into a suitcase and headed off to Belfast. I knew the fight was a risk and I didn't want to take it. Melfah was more than a little put out himself to discover that he'd come all the way from England to give Sammy Storey a decent workout after coming back from a lay-off, only to learn that he had to fight me again. He knew I was going to hurt him and he knew he'd have to earn whatever money he was getting for the fight. But concerned about his careless use of the head the last time we fought, I confronted him in the lobby of the Balmoral hotel on the morning of the fight, told him I would probably be fighting for a world title a couple of months later and didn't want that jeopardised by him cracking me open with his forehead again. He said he wouldn't do it, but I couldn't help but notice how frightened he seemed to be.

Melfah kept his word. He was careful this time and, though it was difficult to feel inspired fighting him, it was a relief just to get out of the ring unscathed. I hurt him, though, made him bear the brunt of all the frustration that had built up in me, until the referee, Barney Wilson, decided he'd seen too much punishment handed out and stepped in between us midway through the fourth round. Though I felt in control from the very first bell, I resisted the temptation to put him out in the first round because I needed a three- or four-round workout to keep me sharp. So the punishment for Melfah was prolonged over ten and a half minutes.

He was hurt a few times in the first round. But the first time he went down was in the second, when I caught him with a right cross that had my full body weight behind it. As I expected, he took his time getting back up again. A young, inexperienced fighter will consider being dumped on his backside as an affront to his ego and will jump back up immediately in indignation, just as the referee is beginning his count. Wily old pros like Melfah take full advantage of the eight seconds, get into a crouch first, and attempt to regain their bearings, clear their minds and get some feeling back in their legs. Trying to get up from knock-down is a bit like trying to stand up from a drunken stupor and Melfah had the intelligence to take his time. But he knew it was only a matter of time until I finished him off. After the second knockdown in the third round, he was not on solid legs, but did well to survive the round, before a left hook returned him to the floor in the fourth. After that, he was seriously hurt and backed into a neutral corner, as I let loose with both hands. To spare him any more punishment, the referee pushed me away from him and waved the fight over. Another win on my record. But not getting cut pleased me more than anything. I went back to the dressing-room and changed quickly to get out in time to see Eamonn beat Duran.

Back at the Balmoral hotel an impromptu party had broken out. My brother Roddy had been playing football for Crusaders against Bangor that afternoon and a large contingent of supporters from Dublin made the trip north for the 'Collins double header'. My supporters and Eamonn Loughran's had swamped a room at the back of the hotel and a singing session was well underway by the time I got back there. Dermot Williams, a family friend, nominated himself as the emcee for the evening and began to introduce people while talking into a Coca-Cola bottle. My brother, Mick, who is a brilliant tenor, gave his rendition of Dicky Rock's 'The Candy Store', and someone else sang 'Dublin Can Be Heaven', before Dermot spotted Barry Hearn walking past. Completely dwarfed by Hearn, Dermot dragged him up to the top of the room, thrust the Coca-Cola bottle under his nose and said: 'Now, Barry, give us a nice Irish song.' For once overwhelmed, Hearn dropped his suave, debonair front for a few minutes while he sang 'The Mountains of Mourne' and took a standing ovation from the crowd.

I noticed that Melfah had slipped into the room unseen and was sitting quietly with a few friends, looking a bit out of place. So I went over, shook his hand and asked him to come over to meet my family and friends. The fight over, I could be nice to him now and start to learn other things about him, apart from his record in the ring and the threat posed by his left uppercut. He'd been adopted as a child and reared on a farm in Wales, news which drew a delighted response from the Irish supporters who were proud that they'd managed to out-sing a Welshman for the evening! It was the first time he'd ever been out on a session with a bunch of Irishmen, but it was an experience he'd never forget.

Before we went our separate ways, I asked him what he was going to do next. He was seriously considering packing it in. Too many beatings take their toll on a body after a while and he wanted to quit while he still had all his faculties. Besides, at thirty-three, he'd long since discarded any hopes he ever had of being a world champion. I still had mine. I thought about him a lot in the days afterwards, about the contrast between us. He seemed to me to be the battle-weary journeyman at the end of a long and unsuccessful career, and I was the experienced pro, who'd achieved a lot in the ring, and was hopefully moving onwards towards another world title shot.

Not that I felt sorry for him as a fighter. Unless you can depersonalise the conflict in the ring, you'll find yourself feeling pity for your opponent as soon as you start to see blood trickling from his nose or a cut around his eye, and you'll start to wonder whether you're doing him serious brain damage and whether he'll talk with a slur in twenty years' time because of the beating you're giving him now. Boxing is business. Nobody was forcing Johnny Melfah to be in there. And somewhere along the line, he'd accepted his role, that he was an 'opponent', there to give upcoming boxers tough fights, but not good enough to beat them. Maybe he liked the image of being a professional boxer, or seeing his name in the newspapers. Or maybe he did it for the money. But nights like that bring home to me the absurdity of my profession. A few hours earlier, I wanted to kill this man, to take his head off his shoulders if that's what it took to get him out of my way. Now, he was another human being whom I could relate to. A man I liked.

WHO WANTS TO BE A MILLIONAIRE?

'Two thousand pounds?' people might say. 'Not bad for a night's work.' Except that it isn't just a night's work. I don't have a salary. Fight nights are my only paydays. If I get injured and am out of the sport for the rest of the year, then £2,000 is my gross salary for the year. And I emphasise the word 'gross', because when Freddy offered me £2,000, he was by no means suggesting that I'd be driving back to Dublin from Belfast £2,000 richer than I was before. Or anything like it. Other people would have to take their cut from it first. It would be a mere shadow of its former self by the time I came to lodge it in my bank account back in Dublin.

The average boxer hands over between 25 percent and 33 percent of his fight purse to his manager and 10 percent to his trainer. So he's left with a little over half. From that, he must pay his sparring partners, his training expenses and his day-to-day living costs. He may have to pay his own hotel bill or plane fare if he's fighting overseas. Then, he'll have to pay income tax and PRSI on whatever is left. Out of every £1 he earns, he'll get between 35p and 40p into his hand. From the £2,000 I'd get to fight Melfah, I'd collect less than £1,000. There were bills to pay – for starters, there was a £500 quarterly phone bill with a lot of Dublin-to-Romford calls on it! Rent, electricity, gas. The kids needed new clothes. And there was another baby on the way.

No, we wouldn't be ready to retire to Rio yet.

CHAPTER 2

A Little Bit of History

DUBLIN BORN, CABRA BRED

I was eight years of age when I threw my first punch in a boxing ring. Though I don't recall who was at the other end of it, I'll never forget his face and, twenty-three years on, the events of that day are still clear in my mind.

A look at our family tree explains why it was inevitable that at least one of us was going to earn his living by fighting. Mum's brother was Jack O'Rourke, the Irish middleweight champion of the 1960s, who went on to become Irish heavyweight champion. Dad was a former Leinster middleweight champion, with a reputation for being a very composed fighter with a heavy punch, and was involved in the very first fight ever to be broadcast live on RTE television. His brother, Terry Collins, another fine middleweight, had an even greater claim to fame: as an amateur back in the 1950s, he'd fought and beaten an English teenager named Reggie Kray. Because both of the Kray twins were highly rated boxers, it was considered quite an achievement at the time. But when they achieved notoriety for their battles outside the ring, Terry's victory became the stuff of legend in the Collins family and, as children, we were all aware that our uncle was one of the few men alive who could say he'd had a fight with one of the Kray twins and won.

Being taught to box was as big a milestone in our young lives as making our first communion or confirmation. My older brothers, Mick and Roddy, had gone before me. And then one night, Dad told me it was my turn. Glowing with pride, I felt like the toughest eight-year-old in the world as we walked up Gardiner Street and stepped downstairs into the dimly lit basement where Maxie McCullough ran the Corinthians Boxing Club. Inside, everything about the gym excited me. The smell of sweat and liniment. The sound of the speed ball beating out a steady rhythm on the bangboard. The sight of a man burying punches into the heavy-bag, as it creaked back and forth on its swivel.

While Dad and Maxie chatted, I noticed a gang of lads on the far side of the gym glowering over at me. They were from the flats around the corner, looked like a rough bunch and didn't seem to think much of their club's newest fighter. They were all skinheads, while I had my hair combed to the side, so I looked more respectable to them, a bit of a softie.

Then Maxie said he wanted me to fight one of them. My first opponent. He was taller, broader and meaner looking than me, and had the backing of the hostile crowd who converged on the ring and started to shout their support. Dad laced my gloves, put the headguard on me and told me to go out and do my best. In the nine minutes that followed, I learned a very valuable lesson – that the toughest kid in the school playground won't necessarily be the best in the boxing ring. I beat him well that night. All of his friends, who'd cheered for him throughout the fight, didn't look so tough and menacing to me now. The 'softie' was supposed to lose, but he'd won. It was my very first fight and already I felt like a champion.

After that, I was smitten. At the age of eleven, I joined Arbour Hill Boxing Club and Dad would come along religiously every Sunday morning to stand and watch me spar and hit the bags. I made good progress too, and when I was sixteen and fighting for the Phoenix Boxing Club, I won my first major championship, the Irish youth heavyweight title. The post-fight banquet was organised by Dad – fish, chips and beans at Wimpy's in Phibsboro.

As a young teenager, I had as many fights outside the ring as I did inside. Not that I was troublesome or that I bullied other kids, I just didn't know how to back down from a confrontation, even against older and bigger lads. I just wasn't a fearful child. I played football for St Brendan's in Grangegorman and the walk home to Annamoe Terrace in Cabra brought me through lonely fields and woods at night, but I was never frightened. Perhaps I was predestined to do something dangerous for a living.

Noticing the flair I showed for drawing, my teachers at the Cabra Tech tried to talk me into becoming an architect. But the way I figured it at the time, if I could leave school and get a job straight away I'd have money and more time on my hands to concentrate on my burgeoning boxing career. So, always my own man, that's what I did. After getting a good Inter Cert, which made my teachers despair all the more that I wasn't staying on, I applied for an apprenticeship at the Guinness Brewery, where Dad worked as a truck driver. And I waited for a reply. One day, Dad came home and said he had a letter for me: they were offering me a job as an apprentice electrician. It was considered the top trade at the time because, as I was told on my first day at the brewery, it involved more use of the screwdriver than the hammer! Being told that his son was going to be a tradesman in Guinness's meant as much to Dad as anything I had ever achieved in the ring.

As a truck driver, he must have been aware of the element of snobbery that existed in the place. The tradesmen looked down on the labourers and the office people looked down on everybody else. Though I was graded second in this class structure, I grew to hate the elitism. Too young and innocent perhaps to understand it at first, it hit me one afternoon when I was walking through a maze of tunnels underneath the brewery. Another employee in a suit was walking towards me. Though I'd never laid eyes on him before, it would have been more awkward not to say hello, because we were the only people in this 200 metre-long tunnel. As he approached, I tried to catch his eye. He'd already seen my overalls though, and fixing his stare at a point just beyond my shoulder, he walked past without even acknowledging me. It bothered me, but somehow I knew, even then, that there was going to be more to my life than trying to climb up some career ladder.

When I was seventeen, Dad died of a heart attack. Losing a parent in your teenage years is all the more devastating when you come from a family that's as close-knit as ours. Dad was its binding force, and without him, things could never be the same for us again. But losing him determined, to a large extent, the kind of person I became afterwards. Without him, I suddenly had to take control of my own life and I became even more strong-willed and assertive. His passing left an enormous void in our lives and the family structure fell apart. Mick and Roddy had already moved out of home. Mum worked as a nurse's aid to support us. Seeing it as my duty as the eldest at home to fulfil the role of 'man of the house', I became very protective of my younger brother Paschal and my sisters. Whenever they were in trouble or needed help, I was there, playing the part of father to them.

But I felt I'd been robbed of something very precious, and boxing didn't interest me any more. At seventeen, I never wanted to get into a ring again. Immersed in so many happy memories, the Phoenix Club gym would never be the same and I couldn't have walked through those doors without breaking down in tears. Too many ghosts. Too many memories of Dad standing at the side of the ring looking on proudly as I sparred. There were other clubs. Dozens of them. But the incentive wasn't there. There was no-one to impress. No-one to be as proud of me as Dad was. No, my inspiration was gone, and I didn't see why I should carry on. I felt like that for a year and a half.

Instead of the boxing gym, my life started to revolve around the technical school in Inchicore, where I was sent for the first year of my apprenticeship training with Guinness's. But, just when I thought I was coming to terms with Dad's death, the year was over and I was back at the brewery again, where all the old memories were revived. Everyone I met seemed to want to tell me how much fondness and respect they had for him. Listening to stories about him, my eyes would fill up with tears. But I loved hearing them and I got to learn great things about him that no-one in the family knew. I discovered that the reason I'd got my apprenticeship in the first place was because of the high esteem in which Dad was held, and also my grandfather, Breff O'Rourke.

Exactly when I rediscovered the spark, I can't say. But I do remember sitting down with Gemma (who was then my girlfriend) to watch one of my heroes, Marvin Hagler, fighting on television and telling her: 'Did you see that mistake he made? I could definitely beat him, Gemma. I'd love to fight him.'

And then one day, the urge came back. The same desire to box I'd felt the very first day Dad brought me to Maxie McCullough's gym on Gardiner Street. I began to think about the secret ambition I had back then, about becoming a world champion when I grew up. I felt that if I could fulfil it, it would somehow bring Dad back. I knew I couldn't return to the old Phoenix Club gym, where there was too much to remind me of him. But Dad had always had a great deal of respect for John McCormack, regarded as one of Ireland's greatest-ever boxers, who ran the St Saviour's Club on Dorset Street. I went along one night and told him that I wanted to box again. He was delighted.

I got myself back into shape and I found working at the brewery was a help as there was no clocking-in and out system and I could sneak out of work in the middle of the morning to go for a run in the Phoenix Park. Work took second place to boxing now and, when tournaments were coming up, I became Guinness's greatest skiver. Out for my run at around 11am. Back for a swim in the company's pool. And after a quick shower, I'd return to the workshop to do ten or fifteen minutes of work.

Whether there would be consequences as a result of my attitude didn't cross my mind. I liked my job, but I loved boxing. A few months later, I won the Irish middleweight title, the same belt my uncle, Jack O'Rourke, had won thirty years earlier. My joy was tinged with some sadness, because I wished Dad could have been there, though winning it made me feel that I'd fulfilled one of the ambitions he had for me. Conscious of our family's proud boxing tradition all my young life, now I knew I was part of it. Something stronger than fish, chips and beans at Wimpy's was in order this time. A crawl of the pubs behind the Bridewell and along the Phibsboro Road was organised. Coming back the following year to defend my title didn't really interest me. I could have gone on and boxed for Ireland at the Olympics in Seoul a couple of years later, but I'd achieved everything I wanted as an amateur. Now I wanted to earn a living from boxing.

My greatest achievement in 1986 was marrying Gemma. On 4 July, America's Independence Day, ironically enough, we both gave up our independence. In the years that followed, she was to be my inspiration and the source of my strength during difficult times. Before we married, we had already decided to emigrate to America to try to find a trainer who was prepared to take me on. Most young boys will grow up dreaming of playing for their favourite football teams. My dream was to train in the same gym as Marvin Hagler and to be taught by his trainers, Pat and Goody Petronelli. I decided to go to Boston and doorstep them one day and tell them I wanted to be a world champion. Maybe they'd be so impressed by my audacity that they'd agree to try to make me the next Hagler.

But first we had to get there. I spent much of that year saving for the airfare but other events overtook me and, as it turned out, I didn't need the money. I'd been picked to represent Ireland in an international against the United States in Boston. Before I left, I handed in my notice at work. I was turning my back on the brewery, a good job, on Cabra, the Phoenix Park and the National Stadium, all in pursuit of my dream to become middleweight champion of the world. I boxed my last amateur bout in the States and stayed on when the tournament was over.

LAND OF OPPORTUNITY

After arriving in Boston in 1986, I looked up a lad from Connemara I'd known during my amateur days. Sean Mannion had taken the same route as I had a few years earlier. He had turned professional in Boston and worked his way up the world ratings. A couple of years earlier, he had lost on points to Mike McCallum in New York when they fought for the WBA light-middleweight title. We sparred for a while in Boston, then he put the word about that there was a promising young Dubliner in town who wanted to turn professional and I waited for Pat and Goody Petronelli to call. Except they didn't. Other trainers and managers did, though. Unimpressed with them, I held out, knowing that the men I wanted were training Marvin Hagler in a gym in Brockton, Rocky Marciano's home-town in south Massachusetts. The big break I was looking for came the night I went to watch Terry Christle fight in Boston. At the party afterwards, I got talking to his brother, Mel, told him about my plans and he offered to introduce me to Goody Petronelli. Feeling a little bit awkward, I shook Goody's hand, while Mel put his hand on my shoulder and said: 'This kid here, he's got great potential. You should work with him.'

'Yeh,' said Goody. 'I'll do that. I'll bring him along and I'll teach him everything.'

Not quite sure whether this was just the same old glib talk you get from boxing people at social functions like these, I decided to put Goody on the spot and asked if I could call down to the gym the following day to train. He said I could. What he and Pat thought of me that first day, I'm not sure. But over time, they began to see that I was serious about making it and that whatever I lacked in skill, I could more than compensate for in sheer effort.

At twenty-two, I found myself working alongside my boyhood idol. The very first day I walked up those three flights of stairs and in through that gym door, there was Marvin Hagler standing in front of me, shaven-headed and grimacing, sweat running down his perfectly shaped body, just oozing aggression and menace. In my youthful exuberance, I told Goody straight away that I wanted to spar with him, but he wouldn't let me. After a couple of visits to the gym, though, I did get to talk to him. He stepped out of the ring after a tough sparring session and picked up the first towel he caught sight of to wipe the sweat from his face and the top of his head. He noticed me looking at him and realised he was using my towel. 'I'm very sorry, is this yours?' he said.

'No, keep on using it,' I said. 'You know, I'll never, ever wash that when you give it back to me.'

We got on well from that moment on. He thought I was wild, because I always wanted to get into the ring and spar with him. There he was, one of the most fearsome fighters in boxing history, the man who cut up Alan Minter so badly it looked as though he was wearing a red mask, the man who hit Tommy Hearns so hard it took them five minutes to bring him round again. Experienced boxers had to be paid big money to spar him. But here was this cocky kid from Dublin constantly following him around, asking: 'Ah come on, Marvin, let's spar with you? Can I?'

'Aren't you scared of him?' people in the gym would ask. Scared? The heavies in Corinthians Boxing Club didn't frighten me. Nor did the walk through the woods back to Annamoe Terrace. Who was Marvin Hagler?

Gemma flew over from Dublin that summer, we set up home in Boston and looked for work to help pay the rent. I took a succession of odd jobs: removals man, builder's labourer, painter and decorator, barman, building porter, electrician's helper, carpenter and bricklayer's labourer, you name it, I did it to help us get by while we were waiting for my boxing career to take off.

Once I started winning fights, I thought, I'd be able to give them up. On my professional debut on 24 October 1986, I stopped Julio Mercado in three rounds and, by the end of the following year, had had seven fights and won them all. Realising my potential, Goody wrote to the US immigration department to try to get my leave in America extended, stating in his letter to them that there was a very real possibility that I would be a world champion one day. The extension granted in early 1988, I signed a three-year contract to fight for the Petronellis and believed that I had at last made a step up into the big time.

But then things began to sour. By the end of December 1988, after spending two and a half years as a pro, I was becoming increasingly unhappy with the standard of my opponents, the amount of money I was getting for my fights and the pace at which things were happening for me. Gemma and I had started our family. The birth of our first daughter, Caoimhe, meant I could no longer look on becoming a successful professional boxer as some childhood ambition or pipe-dream. I had responsibilities and I had to make it work now. But despite having twelve fights since 1986, I was still virtually broke heading into 1989 and had made little progress in the world ratings.

FIRST WORLD TITLE FIGHT 1990

It wasn't until I issued Pat and Goody with an ultimatum to get me some fights against credible opponents for decent money or I was going back home to Ireland that my career really took off. A victory over Paul McPeak, who had been tipped as a future world champion, earned me a shot at the US middleweight title, which I won by outpointing the tough Kevin 'Killer' Watts. Suddenly, I was no longer a mid-ranking undercard fighter any more. After my first two fights in 1989, I was the American middleweight champion and it wasn't only Goody who was tipping me as a future world champion. In my first defence of the title, I beat Tony Thornton, a postman from New Jersey, who, with his shaven head and aggressive style, had been likened to a young Hagler. After a fourth victory over Roberto Rosiles in Las Vegas later in the year, I could no longer be ignored. The world title fight inevitably materialised, against the formidable Jamaican Mike McCallum. But by the time it did, in February 1990, my relationship with Pat and Goody Petronelli had become strained.

While 1989 had been the biggest year of my career, and I didn't know whether I was going to have another like it before I retired, my take-home pay for the year was less than the average industrial worker back home in Dublin was earning. My fights had been staged in Atlantic City and Las Vegas, had been watched by sell-out crowds, sponsored by Budweiser and screened on national television. But I was still having to hang wallpaper, pull pints and lug bricks around building sites to make sure we could pay the rent and eat.

One of the best performances of my career was not enough to beat Mike McCallum in Boston. A little overawed by his reputation at the start, I gave him such a hard time of it through the middle and latter rounds, he said that no amount of money would convince him to give me a rematch. At the time, I thought I'd done enough to beat him, but the judges thought differently. I was too disillusioned with my managers to be angry with the judges. Pat and Goody didn't come near the dressing-room to see me afterwards. Had I won, I was sure they'd have been in there, hoisting me high on their shoulders and popping champagne corks until well into the night. There were arguments they could have made for me. They could have been outside, causing a furore to try to get me a rematch. But their attitude seemed to be: 'Ah well, these things happen. You'll get over it.'

I had lost the biggest fight of my life and was heartbroken. I wasn't a racehorse or a greyhound, I was just a kid who thought his world had ended. I needed consolation, a hug, to be told that I was still the best, in spite of what the judges decided. But the Petronellis, the men I'd dreamed about working with since I was a teenager, weren't there when I needed them most.

Again, there was bitterness over money. Even before the usual cuts, my share of the purse was only $50,000. After everything had been paid, I ended up with about £20,000. Okay, that's more than a year's salary for most people back home, but this was the biggest fight of my life. It might have been the last big fight I ever got. Gemma was just about to have our second child, Stevie. I would not only have to support a wife and two children, but earn enough money to make their futures secure when I quit boxing. And it was obvious to me then that I wasn't going to get the chance while I stayed with Pat and Goody Petronelli. I decided I was getting out. Their remote treatment of me after the McCallum fight was the last straw.

A few weeks later, we flew back to Dublin and, with absolutely no intention of ever returning to Boston, we used the money from the fight and a bit we'd saved to buy a house in Swords. Word spreads quickly on boxing's grapevine and, within a few days, I was talking to several British managers and promoters about resuming my career in Britain. The one who impressed me most was Frank Warren. So one weekend in March, I flew to London to meet him. The contract with the Petronellis was the only stumbling block, but there was a good chance that their share in me could be bought out by a new manager. I found Warren to be a down-to-earth man, very up-front and the deal he offered me was an attractive one. I spent a weekend in London discussing things with him, and he invited me to his executive box at Highbury to see Arsenal play. Leaving the ground afterwards, I bumped into the Irish footballer David O'Leary, who, like me, was going through a period of uncertainty in his career. He was spending most of his time on the substitutes bench, but his manager, George Graham, was refusing to sell him. It was a very, very frustrating time for him. At international level, Jack Charlton had recalled him to the Irish squad after a three-and-a-half year exile, but without first-team football, he didn't think he'd be picked for the World Cup in Italy that summer. I was sure he'd make it and prove them all wrong, and I told him so.

I mulled over the deal that Warren had offered me, but decided not to take it. The training facilities didn't compare to the ones I'd been used to in Boston and it began to dawn on me that the Petronellis weren't going to allow anyone to buy me out of my contract. If I wanted to continue boxing, I'd have to go back to them. I also missed Boston very much and after a few weeks back in Dublin, I was eager to go 'home'. On a whim, I flew to New York and worked for a few days with Floyd Patterson, the former world heavyweight champion, whom I'd met a couple of times before at my fights in Massachusetts. I caught a 'flu virus while I was there and, during the week I spent in bed, had a lot of time to think. Too much time, perhaps. I decided that I was going to phone Pat and tell him that I wanted to come back. Pat and Goody accepted me back with a hug and I felt a bit like the lead in the story of the Prodigal Son. But Pat had a stern warning for me: 'Steve, if you didn't fight for me, I'd have made sure you didn't fight for anyone else.'

But with the same kind of enthusiasm I had shown in the summer of 1986, I got back into training in Brockton and took a job as a barman in Peter and Dick's Tavern on Dorchester Avenue.

It was while working there during the World Cup that my conversation with David O'Leary came back to me. Ireland were playing Romania for a place in the quarter-finals and the match was being shown live in the bar. Extra time had failed to separate the two sides and it was going to be decided by a penalty shoot-out. The two teams were level pegging at 4-4 when Packie Bonner got down low to save Daniel Timofte's weak effort. There was pandemonium in the bar and then a sudden hush fell as everyone realised that, for us to go through to the next round, we had to score our next kick. Who was taking Ireland's fifth? we all wondered. Then, out of the centre circle stepped David O'Leary to make the long and lonely walk to the penalty box. 'O'Leary?' Expressions of disbelief from the experts in the bar. 'He never takes penalties, does he?'

He looked so cool as he placed the ball on the spot and turned to make his run up. The whistle blew. He ran, the Romanian goalkeeper fell to his right and O'Leary hit it to the other side. Goal! People were throwing their pints over one another and I got a right soaking. I looked up at the television and watched O'Leary as he put his arms in the air and sank to his knees, while a herd of players stampeded towards him. To me, that gesture said: You were all wrong!

REBUILDING IN 1990

As I started to rebuild my career again in the gym that summer, David O'Leary was my inspiration – this helped me get through dozens of listless evenings in the gym that summer. Okay, I'd lost a world title fight, but I was good enough to get another. It might only take one victory over a ranked opponent to get it, too.

While I did manage to rekindle the old enthusiasm about boxing, nothing had changed. Pat and Goody just presumed I'd walked out because I wasn't thinking straight after my defeat to McCallum. On the contrary. For the first time in my life, I was thinking straight, facing up to the future, to my responsibilities. That's why I quit. And if I believed that things could ever be the same again between us after the way they had treated me after the McCallum fight, I was deceiving myself. After four years as a professional boxer, I'd lost my innocence. I was no longer the awe-struck child who would have happily fought for nothing just for the honour of being trained by the men who made Marvin Hagler. I wasn't naive any more. And boxing wasn't a game now.

While I still didn't believe that they were capable of getting me the kind of money that I felt I deserved, my contract, which had another nine months to run, meant I had to make the best of a bad situation.

There was a full house at the Boston Sheraton arena that summer to see my return to the ring against Fermin Chirino, a well regarded, New York-based Venezuelan. All of the year's frustrations came out in the ring and the referee stopped the fight in the sixth round after I'd put Chirino down four times. There should have been more at stake for me that night than the money. There was also the promise of a second world title fight. Two days later, in Las Vegas, Nigel Benn was putting his WBO middleweight title on the line against Iran Barkley. Bob Arum, the promoter, had assured me that if I beat Chirino I would fight the winner. In an extraordinary first round, Benn picked himself up off the canvas to put Barkley down three times and win the fight. My next opponent would be Nigel Benn. And I waited for the call from Arum.

That summer, Barry Hearn, who promoted a little-known, flamboyant middleweight from Brighton called Chris Eubank stepped in and made Arum a better financial offer. It was three months before I entered the ring again for my last fight in Boston. This time my points win over Eddie Hall failed to disguise my lethargy.

Though my contract with Pat and Goody had ten weeks to run, they knew I was just killing time until it expired and I felt free to go elsewhere, so I didn't think they'd mind when I headed back to Dublin for Christmas and told them I probably wouldn't be back. They both knew it was coming and I phoned Pat a few days after Christmas to tell him that I was going to look for a new manager and hoped there would be no hard feelings between us. His reaction was one of disappointment. His last words to me were: 'Well, good luck, Steve. And watch out whatever you decide to do, because they're all sharks out there.'

CHAPTER 3

Sweat and Tears

TRAINER KING

After my return from the US I signed to fight for the Belfast bookmaker
and promoter Barney Eastwood. Eighteen months later, after again
fighting unsuccessfully for a world and European title, I joined Barry
Hearn's Matchroom stable in 1992. One of the conditions I laid down
when I agreed to this new arrangement was that I had to be trained by
'whoever works with Eamonn Loughran and Herbie Hide'. I'd seen them
fight on television and knew that they had been very well trained. Barry
said their trainer was Freddy King, who, he said, would be more than
happy to work with me. But I'd have to talk to him myself. Freddy's son
Jason, who worked downstairs in the Matchroom office, took me down
the road to the gym to introduce me to his father. A short man with wiry,
silver hair, a broken nose and a ruddy complexion, Freddy looked
completely disinterested when I introduced myself.

'I'd like to work with you,' I said.

'Naaah ... too busy,' he said, looking around the gym.

I was taken aback.

'I'll get someone else to work with you here in the gym and I'll 'ave
a look at ya from time to time,' he added.

'Look, I can't believe this,' I told him. 'I don't even know you and
I'm already arguing with you. I want *you* to be my trainer. That's the only
reason I've come here.'

Freddy had actually watched tapes of my fights and decided which aspects of my style he needed to work on. But he was asserting himself, letting me know right from the start that he didn't give a damn about who I'd been in the ring with, what I'd won or who I'd been trained by. My past didn't matter any more. There was only the future now. Secretly, he had plans for me.

What had endeared me most to people in the States was my aggressive style, my capacity to stand toe-to-toe with any fighter and trade blows all night, confident in the knowledge that if I could land four punches for every three that hit me, I would win. But too many of my fights had gone the full distance. I was taking a lot of unnecessary punishment. And as I learned to my cost against McCallum, Johnson and Kalambay, scoring boxing matches is as subjective an exercise as judging gymnastics or ice-skating routines. You can't always rely on judges to deliver the verdict you feel you deserve. The only thing you can do is take it out of their hands. What I needed to do was develop a knockout punch, and Freddy said he was going to help me.

The secret of a good punch is in the feet. Developing upper-body strength is absolutely pointless if your stance is wrong when you throw a punch. When I threw one, I had a habit of lifting my back foot off the floor, which meant that none of my body weight was being put behind it. Freddy talked like a physicist at times, teaching me about balance and weight-distribution. 'There is absolutely no reason in the world,' he told me, 'why any man can't punch 'is weight. Ya just gotta be taught 'ow to do it, right? Couple of months wiv me, Steve, you're gonna be knockin' em all aaat, I'm tellin' ya.'

He re-educated me about things I'd neglected, taught me to get down from the balls of my feet and how my feet should be positioned when my punches impacted. He stood at the side of the ring, his arms resting on the top ropes and bawled me out for hours: 'Naaah, Steve, not like that. Do it like this.'

Before long, I began to feel the difference. One afternoon, I was sparring with a very useful middleweight called Lou Gent. I threw one punch just as Freddy had taught me. It was harder than I'd ever hit anyone before and I got a reaction from Lou that I'd never seen from any other opponent. He was just stunned by it.

Working with Freddy was an altogether new experience for me. When I stepped out to fight, I knew that he was behind me in the corner, wanting me to win as much as I did. If I lost, I knew I could count on him not to say: 'Ah well, these things happen in boxing.' He was perceptive and highly knowledgeable about boxing, and a good fight planner. He never bullshitted. If I asked him a question and he didn't know the answer, he'd tell me. Then he'd go home, read his books and come back to me. When I joined Matchroom, I made up my mind that I was going to do everything he told me. Even on the occasions when I found some of his methods a bit questionable, I never told him: 'That's not the way we used to do things in America,' or: 'We didn't do that up in Eastwood's'. Because Freddy didn't care. Reputations meant nothing to him and he'd made that clear the very first day I stepped into his gym.

Freddy had something of a reputation himself. He was a very charismatic man who, a bit like Jack Charlton, was at his most hilarious when he wasn't trying to be funny at all. You could sit down for dinner with him and laugh so much you wouldn't eat a thing. He'd dominate the conversation from starters to dessert with his anecdotes about growing up in the East End of London in the days when the Krays and the Richardsons were carving up the city between them. In his day, getting on if you were working-class meant either becoming a criminal or just being craftier than everyone else. He'd tell his stories without a smile, while everyone else at the table would be fighting for breath.

His short fuse was legendary. Once, he was travelling to the Netherlands with Paul 'Silky' Jones, who was due to fight for the European title in Rotterdam. As they passed through customs at Heathrow airport, a female official stopped Freddy and said she wanted to take a look through his hand-luggage. It was nothing more than a routine check, but Freddy took it as a slight on his character. As she rummaged through his bag, he was becoming impatient, throwing his eyes up to heaven and sighing loudly. Eventually, she pulled out a small steel iron, a tool commonly used in boxing to reduce swelling around fighters' eyes between rounds.

'What's this?' she asked.

Freddy exploded. 'Put that back,' he said, snatching it. And then he continued to grab anything she picked out of the bag. Tired of it all, Freddy eventually went to grab the bag from her and they wrestled for it like two children fighting over a teddy bear, until she finally pressed the emergency buzzer for assistance. Silky looked on in horror as five or six customs officials appeared from nowhere. He was supposed to be fighting for a European title a few days later and had to worry now about whether he'd make bail, let alone make the fight.

But despite his occasional tendency to snap, it was Freddy's cool head that kept me from losing mine during January and February, when I was convinced that everyone was working against me. He was a director of Matchroom and had been Barry Hearn's trainer during his own amateur boxing career. So he held a lot of sway there and when he felt I was becoming so depressed that I was just going through the motions in the gym, he'd go in and argue my case for me. Were it not for him, I'd have walked into Hearn's office, told him what I thought of him and his management and caught the next plane back to Dublin. But there were many afternoons in the gym when Freddy would sit me down and say: 'Listen, Steve, this is the way Barry operates. Now stick with him and it will come, believe me.'

WESLEY SNIPED

It wasn't just for the money that I'd agreed to fight on the Pyatt/Cameron undercard. Before the Melfah fight was sprung on me, I hadn't fought since the end of November the previous year and I didn't fancy the thought of being out of the ring for five or six months before I fought for the title. No, I needed something to keep me ticking over. No-one too difficult, I stressed to Hearn that day in the office. The last thing I needed with my career so delicately poised was an all-out war with some young upstart who wanted to advance his career by beating me. I didn't mind earning crap money for the fight, just so long as it was an easy enough opponent to tide me over while I waited for the big one.

Barry was proving most elusive. I couldn't pin him down anywhere to find out the name of my opponent. With the fight only a week away, I was anxious to know a bit about him, get his record, do a bit of reading on him and watch a couple of videos of him in action. I finally caught up with Hearn in his office one morning. 'Oh, yeh, Steve. I've got your opponent's name 'ere, mate. It's Paul Wesley.'

'Who?' I didn't for a minute mean: Who the hell is Paul Wesley? I knew very well who Paul Wesley was. I meant Who? as in: You can't be bloody serious, Barry!

Wesley was a journeyman. A thirty-one-year-old fighter from Birmingham, whose record of only fifteen wins from forty-two fights didn't do him justice. He'd lasted the distance with both Pyatt and Kalambay and was one of those strangely mercurial fighters who could look sluggish and get knocked out by the most moderate British fighters, but then always seemed to pull out something special against high-ranked opponents. On a good day, he was capable of winning a world title himself. And he had the perfect incentive to beat me, knowing that if he did he, and not I, would be the one fighting Pyatt on 9 April. His was the classic no-lose situation. While the fight was a risk, I knew that if I wasn't capable of beating him, then I had no business being in a world championship ring in the first place. But freak accidents happen in boxing. You can be coasting a fight, walk onto the end of a lucky punch and get counted out. You can get cut by a weak punch. These things happen.

Refusing to fight Wesley never entered my mind. But this wasn't the three- or four-round workout we'd discussed and I thought my purse for the fight should reflect the quality of my opponent and what I was putting on the line. Hearn hummed and hawed, and finally came up with an extra grand.

It wasn't quite as much as I'd hoped for. But at least Hearn had accepted that I was taking a gamble and he might do me a good turn one day. Melfah at a day's notice. Wesley at a week's. That was two favours Hearn owed me.

My fight with Wesley would bring me face to face Pyatt whom I was due to fight next. For a number of weeks, the British tabloids had been running stories that suggested I hated Chris Pyatt. I never said anything to any reporter that could be construed in that way. I didn't know him well enough to form an opinion about him one way or the other. On the couple of occasions I had met him, he seemed quite an affable bloke. We had sat together at ringside at one of Chris Eubank's fights and had a good laugh at Eubank's histrionics in the ring.

The other time I met Pyatt was one afternoon towards the end of January, when I was on my way into the office for one of my regular meetings with Hearn, at which I'd pester him about getting the fight on. But I was told that Hearn was with someone. The 'someone' was Pyatt.

Just then, I heard the door closing upstairs and the sound of footsteps coming down. One of the lads in the office thought it advisable to warn Pyatt that I was downstairs at reception.

'Shit,' I overheard Pyatt say, 'maybe I should nip out the back way.'

But he came down and we shook hands, and had a good laugh over it. He knew that I wasn't the same Steve Collins he'd met before. He had something I wanted and I hated him for not giving me the opportunity to take it away from him. It was fine being friendly with one another while our careers were on parallel courses, but after 9 February as far as I was concerned we were set on a collision course and we couldn't have any kind of normal relationship until our fight was over. I also wanted him to know that, regardless of what was going to be said in the following weeks and regardless of how the newspapers decided to misquote me, I had no personal animosity towards him. It was business. As we weighed in before our fights on 9 February, I stood up and announced it. He looked at me, said he felt the same way, we shook hands and wished one another luck in our fights.

As I expected, my opponent proved a much better match than Pyatt's at the Brentwood Exhibition Centre in Essex that night. I earned every penny of my money, as Wesley took me the full eight-round distance, while Pyatt knocked Cameron out with the first well-intentioned punch of the fight.

Had my fight been scheduled for the full twelve rounds, I was certain I'd have knocked out Wesley inside the distance. He boxed very well and gave me a good workout. He was a very canny opponent, frustrating me for a couple of rounds by using an unorthodox defensive style which involved crossing his arms and keeping his head very low in behind his gloves, his hands protecting both sides of his head and his elbows covering both sides of his body. He used this to try to draw me in and prise open my defence, but he failed. Still, Wesley was awkward to hit at the best of times. Towards the end of each round, he tended to tire, and I landed the combinations of punches that I'd practised with Freddy in the gym. But he was always a danger, especially when he was throwing his wild uppercuts. I felt the wind of one particular delivery as it gusted past my chin, missing me by what must have been only a couple of millimetres in the third round. The only real discomfort he caused me was a hard hook that caught me on the side of the head, burst my eardrum and left me with this muffled ringing in my ear for the rest of the fight. His use of the head was a worry, particularly when he was pushing me backwards onto the ropes, sticking it in my cheek and rubbing it up and down my face.

Although it frustrated me not to be able to put him away, I didn't want to take any risks and never lost control, even during the respite I allowed myself in the middle rounds. The referee awarded me six of the eight, with the other two even. Wesley was ecstatic. He knew he'd put up a good show against me. He left the ring looking like a man who'd just fulfilled his lifetime's ambition. Maybe he had.

Afterwards, he came into my dressing-room to congratulate me and he offered me some words of encouragement too. 'When I fought Pyatt,' he said, 'I wasn't in shape and a few people thought I might have even done enough to snatch the decision. I want you to know I was in shape tonight and I wanted to win so badly. But you were too good. Believe me, you'll have no problem beating Pyatt.'

I came out again in time to watch Pyatt blow away a poor opponent inside three minutes and, interviewed by ITV at ringside afterwards, I told the reporter Jim Rosenthal that I was not only going to beat him when we met, but I was going to knock him out as well.

A MAKE OR BREAK DECISION

A busted eardrum must be one of the most unpleasant injuries a boxer can get. All right, I can say that because I'm lucky enough to have escaped serious injury in the ring. A torn ear lobe, the odd cracked rib, and the occasional cuts around my eyes are about the extent of it. Nothing that can't be cured with a needle and thread and a bit of rest. But when the eardrum pops, it's unfomfortable rather than sore. It's a bit like when you go swimming and a bubble forms inside your ear, and every sound you hear is deadened. The next day, after getting some antibiotics from a doctor in Romford, I headed for Stansted, very much looking forward to going back to Dublin. Getting through the fight without a hitch was a relief and this would be my last weekend home before heading back for four weeks of intensive training for the fight with Pyatt, which I was only now beginning to believe was actually going to happen.

Another reason I was excited about the weekend was that my brother Paschal was fighting as an amateur for the last time at the National Stadium on the Friday night and was entered into the middleweight competition of the senior finals. But, after promising so much in the gym in Romford, he really didn't do himself justice at all that night and we put his defeat in the semi-final down to his inexperience.

I never thought my trip to the stadium that night would erase all thoughts of Pyatt from my mind. But something happened that did. While sitting at ringside, I was approached by a man I'll refer to only as 'The Mole'. An Irishman with very good connections in the business, he has the ears of the most influential people and he hears things, passes information on. More often than not, he knows about offers that fighters are going to receive long before the fighters do themselves. This was one of those occasions. So when he told me that a $125,000 offer was about to be made to me to fight WBC champion Gerald McClellan, I knew that he'd been told by Don King, who promoted McClellan, to try to get my reaction. McClellan's reputation was awesome. One of the heaviest punchers in the world pound for pound, his record of 29 knockouts (20 coming inside the first round) in 31 fights said it all. But, cocksure as ever, I was more than happy to take him on and, having seen him fight, felt I had the perfect plan to undo him.

It's difficult to get your head around the prospect of fighting one of the best boxers in the world in front of a sell-out crowd in Las Vegas when you're sitting in the front row at the National Stadium on a rainy February Friday in Dublin. The more I thought about it, the more reservations I had. Not about the opponent, but I knew that a defeat at this juncture of my career would spell the end and McClellan had retired enough world-class boxers for me to know there was a distinct chance I could lose to him. Still, I believed I had a good chance of winning. But $125,000 wasn't enough. No, I told The Mole, they'd have to come back to me with an improved offer. Before the weekend was out, they did. This time, it was $175,000, which was almost three times more than I was going to get for fighting Pyatt. Now I was interested. But it presented me with something of a dilemma. Pyatt's title was probably the safer bet, not because I thought I was any less capable of beating McClellan, but the Pyatt fight was going to take place in Britain, where I thought I'd have an even chance with the judges. In America, decisions were difficult to get, particularly when it comes to dethroning a very high-profile champion.

It was a very, very tempting offer and I decided to talk it over with Hearn. He was on holidays in Barbados and hadn't left a number where he could be contacted. Eventually I did manage to track him down to his apartment and, forgetting about the time difference, had to apologise when his wife picked up the phone beside the bed to tell me that it was 5.30am.

I told Barry the whole story and he said it was news to him, but that he'd come back to me within twenty-four hours. He didn't phone me. In the meantime, I spoke to Barney Eastwood. Through his partnership with Frank Warren, he had some connections with Don King, who was making the offer. It was a very good one, Eastwood said, and I should seriously consider it. He didn't need to tell me that. While I had no contract with Hearn and was in theory a free agent, I felt I owed it to him to discuss it with him first. A week later, I phoned Hearn, who had just returned from his holidays. He said he'd sent a fax to Don King's office, asking him for details about the McClellan offer, but had received no reply. He told me not to take it seriously, and to concentrate on the Pyatt fight.

But on Saturday, 26 February, Barry phoned me with some bad news. Pyatt, he said, would not be ready to fight on April 16 and wanted a further extension, until the middle of May. I was very angry. I asked Hearn what was going on and he told me not to fret, that if Pyatt hadn't signed the contract by the following Monday, the WBO would strip him of the middleweight title. I knew that something was wrong if Pyatt was stalling so much that the organisation were actually threatening to take the belt from him. I thought there must be some kind of friction between him and Hearn.

The day he was due to sign the contract to fight me, though, my mind was on other things. Gemma, who was fifteen days overdue with our third child, went into labour and gave birth to the latest addition to our family, a girl whom we christened Clodagh.

The following day, Hearn called me at home and asked me rather bluntly: 'Are you straight with me?'

'Of course I am,' I said, thinking he suspected that I was secretly negotiating a deal to fight McClellan. 'Barry, I told you about everything.'

'That's good,' he replied, 'because Chris Pyatt has walked out on me.'

Pyatt, like me, had no promotional contract with Hearn. At any time he was perfectly entitled to get someone else to promote his fights, which he was now doing. Evidently, he felt he would earn more money from fighting me if the entire show was put out to purse offers, which was like a contract being put out for tender. The promoter willing to make the champion the best offer wins the right to stage the contest. The word was that Pyatt had gone to Frank Warren, Hearn's main rival, who now had control of the WBO title. For my own selfish reasons, I was glad that Pyatt was gone. Now, there would be no divided loyalties. Hearn would be fully behind me when I fought for the title. At last, I felt that the only competition I faced was Chris Pyatt in the ring.

As expected, when the fight went out to purse offers on 10 March, Warren won the right to stage it. The date would be announced in the future, he said. My share of the purse would be £50,000, before the usual cuts and expenses were taken out of it. The money wasn't great. But, of course, something much more valuable was up for grabs.

CHAPTER 4

The Night of My Life

MIND GAMES

Muhammad Ali didn't invent it. But he certainly mastered it.

'You're so ugly,' he told Sonny Liston, 'that when you cry, the tears run down the back of your head.'

'You can't talk properly,' he told Joe Frazier.

'You ain't nothing but an Uncle Tom,' he said to Floyd Patterson.

It's the art of upsetting another fighter to the extent that he's too angry or too frightened to fight properly. It doesn't always work, of course. Not every boxer has the charisma and sharp mind of Muhammad Ali, as well as the skills to back up his bravado. So other things are used to unnerve fighters before they get into the ring.

It would be easy to develop a paranoia about these things, but there have certainly been times when persons unknown have gone to extraordinary lengths to try to ensure that I lost even before I had my gloves laced.

Three nights before I fought Reggie Johnson in New Jersey in 1992, my sleep was interrupted at regular intervals by the phone on the bedside table ringing. Whenever I answered it, there was nobody on the other end. I asked the hotel receptionists whether there was a fault with the line to my room. There wasn't. The following night, it continued. Now, while I've never believed that Johnson himself had any part in it, someone was very determined to see to it that I didn't get any proper sleep before the fight.

Then there was the trip to France the previous year to fight Jean Noel Camara in Brest. After being put in the wrong dressing-room twice, I spent half an hour before the fight wandering around backstage, looking for somewhere to get changed. Finally, on the way to the ring, an official, for a reason that was never explained to me, told me I'd have to change my gloves. Absolutely incensed, I refused, and then spent a further ten minutes in the ring, kicking dust and shivering with the cold, until Camara finally decided I'd waited long enough for him and came out.

Inexperienced fighters will have their hearts broken by this kind of treatment. But I'd been in the business long enough to expect it. Nothing, though, prepared me for the kind of things that happened to me in the weeks before my fight against Pyatt. It started with the date, which had already been changed three times. The first had been set for 16 April in Pyatt's home town of Leicester. It was put back to 30 April. Then it was changed to 25 May. One afternoon towards the end of February, sitting in Barry's office, I said: 'Well, let's hope that's the last date change, eh?' Just as the words left my mouth, the phone rang. Barry frowned, '*Wha*...? You're jokin'? Not again!'

He turned to me. 'You're not gonna believe this, Steve. They've gone and changed it again.'

The boxing writers from the newspapers back in Dublin had been on to say they'd been told it was switched again. May 11 was the new date. Barry was as angry as I was and he phoned Warren's office to find out what was going on. No, said Warren, the date had not yet been set, and wouldn't be until after Easter. So I'd just have to wait.

Both Warren and Pyatt knew that this would work to my disadvantage. They knew the effort I had to put in to make the middleweight limit. Unlike Pyatt, there wasn't a two- or three-pound difference between my fighting weight and my 'walking around' weight. My natural weight is around 12 stone, 6lbs. Fighting at middleweight my weight had to be 11 stone, 6lbs. I had to sweat off a stone in the gym before I fought. Without a definite date on which to focus, I faced a bit of a dilemma. If I threw myself into training immediately, I might discover after Easter that the fight wasn't until the end of May and I'd be knackered by the time I got into the ring. On the other hand, I could pace myself in the gym and then have a mid-April date sprung upon me. Then I'd have to work doubly hard to make the weight limit and could be completely drained of energy by the time I came to fight.

All I could do was keep up my schedule in the gym. Every day, I went through the daily drudgery of skipping rope, shadowboxing, hitting the heavy bag, working the speedball and sparring, until, in the middle of April, we were finally given the date and venue. Just as the Irish boxing writers had heard, it would take place on 11 May, but not in Leicester at all. The venue would be Sheffield's spectacular Ponds Forge International Sports Centre, which was built by the local city council as the main venue for the World Student Games three years earlier. The thought of fighting in Sheffield appealed to me a lot more than Leicester. While the two cities were close to each other and Pyatt would still have his travelling support, it wasn't his home town. I remembered that Paul 'Silky' Jones, my old friend who sparred quite regularly down in Romford, lived there. I decided to give him a call to see if he could rustle up a bit of local support for me.

A lunchtime press conference was arranged for 18 April in Sheffield. But by the time Frank Warren told me about it, I had already organised a sparring session for that afternoon down in Romford. And anyway, I was feeling the beginnings of a 'flu, which was becoming a bit of an occupational hazard for me because I had to take off so much weight and so drastically.

It's not natural for a body to suffer what I put mine through. As well as working myself into exhaustion in the gym, I wasn't eating proper meals because of my concern about keeping my weight down. So naturally, I was more susceptible to any 'flus, colds and bugs that were doing the rounds in Romford. Feeling very unwell and completely drained of energy, I took to my bed early on 18 April and didn't get up again for a couple of days. But if my condition wasn't bad enough, another surprise was making its way to me through the fax machine in the office next door. It came from Frank Warren to Barry Hearn:

Dear Barry,

Re Steve Collins

I have been informed by a reliable source that the previous management of the above fighter, the Petronelli brothers, have obtained a judgement against Steve Collins with regard to monies due to them. Apparently, the judgement has been registered in this country. I understand the amount is far in excess of Collins' purse. My concern is that he is definitely going to fight on 11 May, 1994. Despite being given four days notice, he did not attend Monday's press conference. I thereby require written confirmation from Collins that he is definitely fighting on 11 May and that we're not wasting our time.

PAT, GOODY AND THE $250,000 QUESTION

Just how I came to owe almost a quarter of a million dollars to Pat and Goody Petronelli is a question that would tax even the most astute of legal minds. Unless I completely misjudged his mood on the phone, Pat sounded as though he'd accepted my decision, albeit reluctantly, to leave back in 1991. A couple of months after I walked out with only a matter of weeks to go in my contract, word got back that he was very annoyed and was going to do everything he could to challenge me.

I was too enthusiastic then about making a new start to worry about Pat's threats and, through my former agent Fintan Drury, I arranged a meeting with Barney Eastwood, the Belfast bookmaker and boxing promoter who had managed the careers of Barry McGuigan and Dave McAuley. Early in 1991 after I'd returned from the States, we drove up to meet him at a hotel close to the border on the Republic side. After dinner, I was asked to leave the table while Drury and Eastwood discussed a deal. I spent half an hour or so kicking my heels outside until they finally emerged. Eastwood got into his car and headed back towards

Belfast, while Drury filled me in on the details on the drive back to Dublin. Pleased with the terms he was offering, I was happy to sign an eighteen-month contract with him as soon as my agreement with the Petronellis had officially expired.

The deal Eastwood offered me included a European title fight against Michael Watson. We called a press conference in Dublin to announce details. The fight was to take place on 17 March 1991, a date that had been deliberately chosen, not just because it was St Patrick's Day, but because my contract with my former managers was due to expire at midnight on 16 March. That was my interpretation of it anyway. The Petronellis and their attorney, Morris Goldings, argued that it didn't expire until midnight the following day. But whatever the correct date, my view was that it should all have been immaterial. The fight fell through. My first fight under Eastwood didn't take place until 11 May, two months later, when I knocked out Kenny Snow in three rounds in Belfast. My contract with Pat and Goody had expired eight weeks previously. So I was in the clear. Or so I thought.

Their attorney would later claim that my appearance at the press conference in Dublin had violated a clause in the contract which precluded me from allowing my name to be used 'in any commercial enterprise whatsoever without first obtaining the permission of the manager'. That was trivial enough, I figured. Then they claimed that they had 'executed' and 'negotiated and obtained' a fight for me on 10 May, 1991, against IBF middleweight champion Michael Nunn. I have never seen any evidence that Nunn had ever agreed to this particular fight and certainly I had never signed a contract for it. The proposed agreement, in fact, bears only one signature, that of Bob Arum, chairman of Top Rank promotion company who were to promote the event. I didn't need to be reminded that this kind of document could be worthless and, to prove it, I had an almost identical one in which Arum promised me a fight against Nigel Benn which never materialised. By any stretch of the imagination, the fight could not be said to have been 'negotiated and obtained'.

However, the dispute with the Petronellis lost me the sympathy of the US media by depicting me as an ingrate who had bled what he could out of two of boxing's most respected figures and then walked out. The growing media hostility towards me was summed up in the 10 February edition of the *Boston Globe*. It claimed that the Petronellis had built me 'from an unknown club fighter with a punch so light he couldn't break a dollar if he had four quarters in his fist, into a middleweight contender in line for his second title shot in less than 12 months'.

While the argument was becoming an emotive one, the legal question was simply whether I had violated my contract by allowing my name to be used in connection with a promotion that never took place. And if that was the case, just what kind of price could be put on it. When the case came to court in 1993, the Petronellis claimed, according to a memorandum from Chief Judge Joseph L Tauro of the US District Court, that 'media coverage of the defendant's action caused the plaintiffs significant injury' in Massachusetts. But I wasn't in Massachusetts at the time. I was back in Ireland, training in Belfast and trying to forget about the whole mess.

I was at a loss to explain how the media coverage had damaged the Petronellis. They seemed to have done well in getting their points across in the newspapers. A few days after the court proceedings, I received a letter from the Petronellis' lawyer, Morris Goldings. Couched in the usual expensive legal-speak, the bottom line of the letter was that he could make it all go away if I extended my management contract with the Petronellis and Top Rank, Inc. It concluded: 'If you refuse to proceed in this manner, I am authorized to institute litigation against you ...'

Hot air, I thought. Surely any judge worth his corn would find their case as flimsy as I did. Fintan Drury hired the Boston law firm Goodwin Proctor and Hoar to fight for me. My case was handled by Andrew Shipley, who admitted that he found dealing with boxing people to be a very 'educational' experience. 'It was my feeling then and is my feeling now that the plaintiffs' case was without any real merit,' he said in a recent interview with the *Boston Herald*. Rather than challenging the claim that a breach of contract had taken place, Shipley contested the case largely on procedural grounds, claiming I hadn't been served at my legal residence when the case first came to court in 1991.

The Petronellis were already out to rectify this. When I returned to the States for my second world title fight, against Reggie Johnson, in April 1992, their legal people went to great lengths to serve me the writ again. Because of all the bogus phone calls I'd been getting, I changed to another hotel room a few days before the fight. The man who ended up getting mine returned to his room after being out one day to discover that a writ with my name on it had been shoved under his door. It hadn't been properly served, of course, but it alerted me to trouble. Their second attempt the following day produced some unforgettable scenes in the hotel foyer and forecourt. Gemma and I finished our dinner in the hotel restaurant and were waiting for the elevator when someone called my name. I turned around and a man with a suit was standing there. 'Hey, Steve,' he said, 'I have something for you.' He tried to shove a piece of paper into my hand but I threw my arms in the air, refused to touch it, turned around and started to walk away. Hotel security were on the case immediately. Two guards came over and, as they manhandled him out of the building, he threw the piece of paper on the floor and screamed: 'Well, we know where you'll be on Wednesday night.' Wednesday was the day I was due to fight.

Quincy Taylor, my sparring partner, picked up the piece of paper.

'What'll I do with it,' he asked.

'I'm not touching it,' I said. 'Throw it in the bin.'

A little shaken, I wanted some air and Gemma and Quincy joined me for a short walk. Before we got out of the hotel grounds, the man was drove past and gave us a dirty look. I bent over, as if to pick up something, and threw an imaginary rock at his car. It skidded to a halt and he jumped out. At once, he was in front of me and, as he whipped back his jacket, I couldn't believe what was sticking out of his belt. It was a gun. He's going for it, I thought. Fuck, he's gonna shoot me! You hear so many stories about this kind of thing in America. He reached instead for his back pocket and produced a badge – a police badge. 'Do you know what this is?' he asked. 'I could have you arrested for what you just did.'

'You're a cop?' I said, starting to regain my composure. 'You know you're not supposed to be moonlighting by serving writs on people. It's illegal, isn't it?'

More than a little taken aback at my knowledge of the law, he suddenly became uneasy, got back into his car without saying another word and got out of the hotel grounds as quickly as his expensive car could carry him. Quincy hurled a torrent of abuse after him.

I was satisfied that the writ hadn't been served but obviously, as events unfolded, the courts in the US believed that it had. After I'd lost to Johnson, I didn't particularly care. It was a very upsetting time for me and I was too tired to argue and just totally disillusioned with boxing anyway. I returned to Ireland and wished the whole business would go away. It was best, I thought, just to bury my head in the sand. Later I realised that this was very, very stupid.

Because he was acting as my manager at the time, Barney Eastwood had also been named as a co-defendant in the original lawsuit. He got Philadelphia lawyer Jimmy Binns, who is also senior counsel for the WBA, to handle his case. The action against Eastwood was different to the one I faced. I was being sued for a violation of my contract and he was just an alleged party to it. In June 1993, Binns successfully persuaded the US District Court in Boston to dismiss all proceedings against Eastwood. Less than three weeks later, Judge Tauro ordered that I had 'defaulted for failure to file a status report', which, in layman's terms, means that the Petronellis won the case against me because I had not turned up in court to defend myself.

The judgement he entered was astonishing. I was to pay them $165,534.15 plus costs, plus 12 percent interest for every year they waited for it. It amounted to $219,031.15. The facts of the case hadn't even been argued in court, but it didn't matter. As Judge Tauro's clerk, Mary Coughlan, said in a letter to my solicitor later in the year: 'The judgement in no way reflects the merits of the case. The merits of the case were never litigated. Collins was defaulted for failure to follow the court's procedures, specifically failing to provide a status report. That's pretty much standard procedure.'

MORE MIND GAMES

By March 1994, the amount they claimed I owed them was deemed to have reached $244,231.15. There was no way I could or would pay the Petronellis that kind of money. I didn't have it and, anyway, I am convinced that, had the case been argued in open court, they wouldn't have been awarded a cent. The situation was that, legally, they'd now be entitled to seize my share of the purse as a down-payment on what the court had awarded them if I fought in the United States. But the judgement stood only in the US. As long as I continued to fight in Europe, they couldn't touch my money. As I lay in bed, trying to recover from the 'flu, that belief was shaken by the fax that came through the machine in Barry Hearn's office next door. According to the information supplied by Warren's 'reliable source', they were now entitled to take any money I earned from boxing in Britain too. They were entitled to take my money for fighting Pyatt and then any other money I earned in the future until the full amount was paid.

Panic stations. How the hell could the Petronellis obtain a judgement in Britain when I hadn't even been given a chance to defend myself in a British court? The story had broken back in Dublin that I'd have to fight Pyatt for nothing. My world title fight, as far as everyone back in Ireland was concerned, was off. Martin Breheny from the *Irish Press* and Tom Cryan from the *Irish Independent* were first on the case and spent the entire day trying to contact me. I was too upset to talk to them. That night, RTE's Six-One News announced that the fight was almost certainly off because the Petronellis were going to take my purse. Feeling a mixture of worry, confusion and anger, I didn't sleep at all that night. The following day, I phoned my solicitor in Dublin, who rubbished the story. No judgement had been obtained against me in Britain, he said. On the contrary, his most recent discussions with the Petronellis' lawyers had been very productive and they indicated that they would settle for a portion of the original court award.

Still struggling to recover from the 'flu and from this latest shock, I returned to Dublin for a short break. It would be my last before the fight. When I got back to Romford, Barry persuaded me to travel up to Sheffield for another press conference that had been arranged for Tuesday, 26 April. 'They're causing bloody murder over you not going to the last one, so you'd better go up,' he said. So I phoned my old friend Silky Jones and he met me at the station.

In my eight years in professional boxing, I had met all too few people like Silky. He's one of a rare breed, a sincere guy who hasn't allowed the sport to embitter him. A man who believes, as I do, that boxers come first, ahead of promoters, managers, trainers, everyone. Approaching a fight, the company you keep is all-important. You need companions who know when to talk to you and when to shut up, when to offer encouragement and advice, and when to listen. During the short time I'd known him, Silky had never put a word wrong. We had much in common. He was also a middleweight, had children and knew what it felt like to be away from them for a long time. He had a very, very wide knowledge of boxing, but could talk about anything you wanted to. When I beat Pyatt, I decided, I was going to invite Silky to be part of my team as I prepared to make my first defence.

On the day of the press conference, we went for a short run around Sheffield, during which Silky told me he'd arranged for a fairly sizeable party of supporters to be there to cheer me on. He seemed very amused about something and it wasn't until I met my 'Irish' supporters that I discovered why: they were all either black or Asian, all local lads and all well over six feet tall. It would be such an intimidating experience, Silky explained, for Pyatt, a black man fighting in his own country, to watch an Irishman burst into the press conference with a large entourage drawn from the local black and Asian communities. Silky, you're a genius, I thought. I couldn't wait to see the look on Pyatt's face.

As it happened, I didn't get to. Pyatt didn't turn up this time. Nor did Frank Warren. Retaliation for my no-show the last time perhaps? Their representatives were there to ensure that the mind-games continued. I told the journalists how happy I was to be in Sheffield, how well my training was progressing and how confident I was of taking the title from Chris Pyatt. Then I was asked about my efforts to make the middleweight limit in time for the fight. No, it wouldn't be a problem, I said, even though, as I get older, it's necessary for me to work that bit harder to shed the pounds. 'While we're on the subject of weight,' I said, looking over at one of Warren's men, 'when will the weigh-in be taking place?'

Now, I must confess, I was being more than a little mischievous here. The previous day, I'd received a fax from the WBO which said that, under new rules, the weigh-in for the fight would have to take place the day before it was staged, 'between 6pm and 10pm'. This was the first sign that things were starting to go my way. A weigh-in twenty-four hours before the fight was to my advantage, because as the bigger and heavier of the two fighters I had to work harder to make the limit and was a lot weaker by the time I stepped on the scales. During the twenty-four hours between the weigh-in and the fight, I could eat what I wanted and put a few pounds back on, so I'd be strong again. I knew this, but asked the question just to see what reaction Pyatt's people would give.

'The weigh-in will take place on the day of the fight as usual,' one of them answered.

'Well, that's funny,' I said, 'because I've got a piece of paper here from the WBO which seems to contradict you.'

He read it closely, then agreed it would be the day before. In the pre-fight psychological battle, I'd scored my first direct hit. Pyatt and Warren hadn't been there to see it, but my journey to Sheffield hadn't been a wasted one after all. I said goodbye to Silky and headed back to Romford to complete my training, believing now that attempts outside the ring to rattle me were based on fears of what I might do inside it.

Romford is best described as a well-to-do suburb of London. An ancient market town in Essex, it has a very distinct cockney flavour and its large estates are home to thousands of resettled East Enders who made a few bob and moved out. Along with The 'Ammers – or West Ham United, as the rest of the country knows them – boxing is one of the East End's greatest loves. Because Pyatt's trainer, Jimmy Tibbs, grew up not far from Romford, and because many of his friends still lived in and around the area, I became very wary of people coming into the gym to watch me train. I'd always ask Freddy: 'Do you know that guy there?' And if he didn't, I'd ask around the gym: 'Is he with you? What does he want here?'

One Saturday afternoon, two men, who sounded as though they'd just stepped out of the set of EastEnders, came in and sat down to watch me spar. They must have noticed the suspicious glances I was throwing them, because one of them eventually piped up: 'Aw roight, Steve, 'ow's it goin', mate?'

'Not too bad, lads. Are you all right?'

'Great, thanks.'

And then, without any degree of subtlety whatever, they started to interrogate me about my preparations for the fight. As it happened it wasn't a serious session, so I let them stay, answering their questions with a Yes, No or the odd grunt and, after an hour or so, they left.

Three days later, they returned again. In they walked, as I pulled on my gloves and got ready to spar. All smiles, they greeted me like a couple of old family friends. Now, I didn't for one minute believe that these two East End boxing enthusiasts were all that fanatical about an Irish fighter. I mean, even my family and closest friends couldn't face the monotony of watching me train for a couple of hours. I couldn't take the risk. I told them to leave, that this was a private session. Their faces dropped and they looked me up and down, as if to say: Who the hell do you think you are? and stormed out. Another man from the East End who was in the gym at the time reckoned I was spot-on with my suspicions, but I never did find out who they were or why they were there.

The psychological sparring continued. On 5 May, less than a week before the fight, I brought up the subject of my expenses with Frank

Warren's office. It must be explained that it's customary for a fight promoter to pick up the bill for both boxers' travel and accommodation. In my eight years as a professional, this has always been the case. But the tradition was being dispensed with for this fight. My train fare and hotel expenses were my own affair, the woman in Warren's office explained. Not only that, neither would I be reimbursed the money I'd spent getting to Sheffield for the press conference they'd asked me to attend. This really pissed me off, but I made up my mind not to let it upset my preparations. It just made me all the more determined to win the fight and wipe that self-satisfied grin off Frank Warren's face.

A few days before the fight, Barry Hearn came to me and, for the first time, asked me to sign something to say that he was my manager. It wasn't necessary, he said, to sign a standard contract, just a simple statement that would be officially witnessed, simply to say that he would be my manager and promoter for the next eighteen months. I did it.

There were other things on my mind as well as boxing. Just because I'm away from home most of the time doesn't mean I've abandoned my role as a husband and father. Thoughts of Pyatt were occupying my mind about 80 percent of the time, but there were family matters that had to be taken care of too. One afternoon, a week before the Pyatt fight, I had to phone the principal of a school in the Castleknock area where we wanted to enrol Stevie for the following term. Gemma and the children weren't living in the area at the time, but I explained on the phone to the headmaster that we were going to build a house there and would be renting one nearby until it was completed. If my nightly phonecalls from Gemma and the monotonous daily routine of wake-run-breakfast-laundry-gym-telly-bed didn't convince me how much I was missing home, then Roddy Doyle's *The Family*, which was shown on British television that night, did. There isn't a place in the world like Dublin, I thought, and the programme had captured the spirit, the character of the city perfectly. Yes, I missed Dublin very much.

Four weeks before the fight, Freddy King and I wrote the script. He knew how Pyatt would approach me. He'd try to overwhelm me with sheer aggression, hitting me hard and early, because fighters have this mistaken belief that I can be hurt easily. But he was definitely going to try to knock me out. If this was Pyatt's strategy, he'd been badly advised. The only punch to put me down in my professional career was a sucker shot to the solar plexus from Kevin Watts, whom I went on to beat quite comfortably on points. I'd never been hurt badly enough in the ring to feel in danger. I found it inconceivable that a fighter of Pyatt's experience could believe that a natural light middleweight, as he was, could overpower a much heavier man who'd traded shots with some of the biggest hitters in the middleweight division. I'd expected him to move for the entire fight, knowing that I'd have to come after him and take the title from him. 'Nah!' said Freddy, 'he's frightened that you'll catch up with 'im eventually and knock him out, so he wants to get to you before you get to him.'

Freddy spotted Pyatt's Achilles' heel. It was his tendency to drop his left hand low when he threw a right, leaving the left-hand side of his head exposed for about a second. My game-plan was to keep jabbing and then, when he eventually dropped his left, to throw a right over the top. Freddy is one of the most perceptive people in the sport. I watched some videos of Pyatt's past fights and he was right, Pyatt did have this tendency to drop his left low. And I was left shouting at the television: 'His guard's down, hit him ... HIT him ... NOW!'

GOOD BLOODLINE, BAD BLOOD

I'm Irish. Nobody's ever been left in any doubt about that. Taking out British citizenship would have been an enormous help to my career when I joined Matchroom, but changing my nationality was something I wasn't prepared to consider. For several years, I was the only active boxer in the world to carry an Irish boxing licence. Whenever I fought in America, I was always introduced as 'Irish' Steve Collins. When I began to get exposure, I had a shamrock sewn on to the left side of my shorts and three castles on to the right. A tricolour was always carried in front of me into the ring and the music that heralded me always had an Irish theme, whether it was U2's 'I Still Haven't Found What I'm Looking For', The Commitments' 'Mustang Sally' or House of Pain's 'Jump Around'.

So when I got a look at the programme for the Pyatt fight, I should have been delighted that they'd gone to the trouble of printing a green, white and orange backdrop behind my photograph on the cover. Behind Pyatt's picture was a Union Jack. That didn't please me at all. The colours, I felt, were being used to assert Pyatt's identity, his Britishness, and to alienate me, by pointing out that I was the foreigner fighting a Briton on his own patch. Pyatt would have the backing of the crowd and that would offer him another edge. It doesn't matter what you're talking about, whether it's boxing, the Eurovision Song Contest, or the strength of our currencies, Ireland *versus* Britain tends to bring out these very strong nationalistic tendencies in people. It's a shame really, because I think Irish people and English people go to watch sports events for the same reason, to see a good contest, not to become jingoistic about it.

The fight posters, thousands of which had been stuck on billboards and lampposts all over Sheffield, claimed that I was fighting out of Dublin. This was incorrect. I was fighting out of Romford in Essex. But if Warren thought I was going to try to play down my nationality, he was wrong. When I saw the programme, I went to a local tailor in Romford and asked him to make me a pair of shorts from a piece of green and blue tartan material I'd bought, and got him to print the words 'Celtic' on the front and 'Warrior' on the back. Now I was undeniably Irish and proud of it. Before I left for Sheffield, I needed a haircut. So I went to the barber around the corner from the gym. 'Usual?' he asked, the 'usual' being a flat top with the sides cut very short.

'Yeh,' I said, 'but could you also shave a shamrock on either side?'
He laughed.
'I'm serious,' I said. 'Can you do it?'
When I finally convinced him, he drew a shamrock onto a piece of

cardboard and his wife cut it out to make a stencil. As he went to work, still a little bemused, I explained about the programme and the posters that were hanging up in Sheffield. His own roots were in Scotland, he said, and he considered it an honour to prepare a 'fellow Celt' for battle. Just as he finished the last leaf on the second shamrock, word was sent down that we were running late and would have to leave for Sheffield immediately if we were going to make it in time for the weigh-in.

Even with the bitterness over the delay in announcing the fight day, the fax about the Petronellis and the refusal to pay my expenses, I felt no personal animosity towards Chris Pyatt. However, I discovered at the weigh-in, that he mistook the gesture I'd made before his fight with Mark Cameron, when I had shaken his hand and we wished one another luck. When we met at the weigh-in the night before our own fight, he wanted another handshake. I pulled away from him. 'No,' I said. 'I'm sorry, Chris, nothing personal, but it's fight-time now.'

Thinking I was being ignorant just for the sake of it, he mumbled something about how he was going to knock me out, which I didn't like. 'What the fuck did he say?' I asked, and tried to get over to him to confront him. 'What did you say?' I was ready to fight there and then, but Silky and his friends calmed me down, while Pyatt's trainer Jimmy Tibbs and Freddy started hurling insults at each other in East End accents. Nastiness was starting to sneak in now.

After the weigh-in, I asked about getting tickets for my wife and my mother, who were among a group of about sixty people flying in from Dublin for the fight. Again, the custom is that both fighters are provided with two ringside tickets. Not this time, though. No, I was going to have to pay for them myself. And they were £100 each. Never before, not even since my earliest professional days, had I experienced such treatment.

Some petty squabble over tickets wasn't going to break my spirit and, in the hotel, the excitement was beginning to mount. People were starting to arrive from Ireland. A crowd of about thirty-five had been there to watch me weigh in a pound under the limit and the sense of expectation was palpable. There were so many friends there who'd shared my dream from the start, lads who'd saved, hocked and borrowed to travel the world to watch me fight, who'd been there on the good and bad nights in Boston, Brest, New Jersey, Belfast, Verbania, Las Vegas, Cardiff and London. Lads I'd grown up with in Cabra had come, along with a large party from Walshe's pub in Stoneybatter. As I stepped off the scales, there was a huge roar: 'GO ON, STEVE!'

The nitpicking continued. Pyatt's trainers insisted that I went to the rules meeting. Their concern this time was about my 'beard'. Quite often before a fight, I let about five days of growth build up and then shave it off before I get into the ring. This time, though, I intended to wear a goatee for the fight, but Jimmy Tibbs claimed, rather ludicrously, that it would lessen the impact of Pyatt's punches on my chin – another trivial mind-game. 'It comes off,' he said, 'right?'

'No, I want it to stay on,' I said.

'Look, you're not in America now. You're in Great Britain and British rules say it comes off.'

'Marvin Hagler wore a goatee throughout his career ...'

'Look, I just told you, you're not in America now.'

'No, if you knew your boxing, Jimmy, you'd know that he wore it when he fought in Britain too,' I said. 'But I won't argue with you. I'll take it off. I'm better looking without it anyway ...'

None of the mind-games had worked. I had a nice meal, slipped off to bed early and slept soundly.

The next day, the day of the fight, just seemed to disappear. Different fighters have different pre-fight rituals. I like solitude, to lie down for the afternoon, sometimes to sleep, but most often to gather my thoughts, think of my game-plan, think about things that could happen in the ring that night and how I'd cope with them. What if my nose gets broken? Well, I'll breathe through my mouth. What if I get cut badly? Well, I'll hang on for dear life until the end of the round, when Freddy will slop some grease on it and try to close it up. What if I lose? There's no way I'm going to lose.

I spent the afternoon in a different hotel room, where no-one could contact me, until the early evening, when I allowed my brothers and a few friends to come in to talk to me. They'd all been through the routine with me so many times before, they know what to say to me and what not to.

As it came close to time, an aunt of ours, who lives in Birmingham, dropped in with a gift. I've never had photographs of myself as a baby – I don't really know why. She brought me a picture of myself when I was nine months old and, for ten or fifteen minutes, I couldn't stop myself looking at it. I became very emotional. I couldn't see myself in it at all, I just kept seeing my own son. And this moment stood out for me. It was the moment I realised that I wasn't just representing my country or myself out there. I was representing my family too.

About fifty or sixty people had gathered at the hotel to see me off and, as we climbed into the limousine, it was great to hear the Dublin accents:

'Knock the head off him, Steve!'

'See ye back at the party!'

'Up the Dubs!'

As we drove towards the Ponds Forge International Sports Centre, I didn't need reminding that this was the most important fight of my life. I wondered whether I'd be playing the part of the good loser again at the end of the evening, the same part I'd played in Boston after losing to Mike McCallum, in New Jersey after my defeat to Reggie Johnson, and in Italy ... For some reason, that evening in Verbania, northern Italy, in October 1992 came to mind. I was certain I'd done enough to beat Sumbu Kalambay that night, but he was allowed to keep his European title belt. It was my second fight of the year and my second loss, coming just six months after my defeat by Johnson, and my career seemed to be over. Two world title fights and one European was more chances than most fighters get in their careers. After the fight that night I'd had to play the part of the good loser, which I hated. During the drive to the arena in Sheffield I decided that if I had to do it again this evening, it would be for the last time. If I lost, I decided, I was going to retire, because I couldn't go through another three years of this kind of strain to build up my rating again. Tonight, it was everything or nothing.

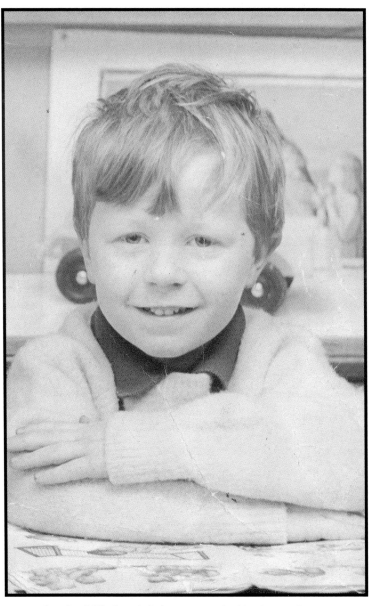

**Angelic child: there is little to suggest in this picture of me at
five years old how I'd go on to earn my living.**

**One of my earliest victories was at a Tarzan look-alike competition
at Butlins holiday camp when I was eight years old.**

ABOVE: With my greatest inspiration, my father Paschal, at Portmarnock beach in 1967. BELOW: Posing for a photograph at the Thomas à Becket gym in London with my friends from St Saviour's boxing club.

Showing off the Irish Junior light-heavyweight title in 1984
and the shiner I picked up on the way to winning it.

ABOVE: Wedding Bells – Gemma and I are married at Aughrim Street church in 1986. BELOW: Standing with my workmates at the Guinness brewery in 1986, contemplating the quickest escape route up to the Phoenix Park!

ABOVE: A treasured moment – meeting one of my boyhood heroes, Marvin Hagler, in Boston. BELOW: Another step on the way to the top – celebrating a victory with Pat and Goody Petronelli.

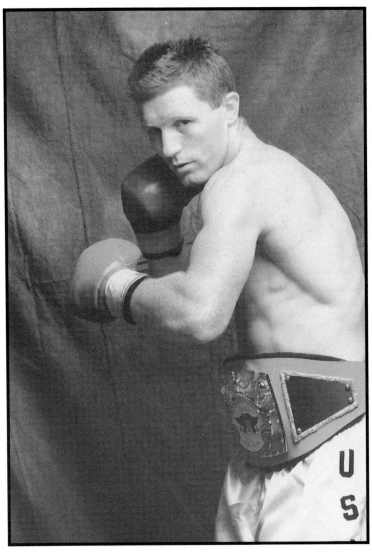

**Proudly displaying the US middleweight title belt
I won from Kevin Watts in 1989.**

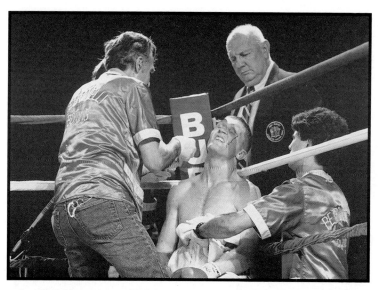

An official keeps a watchful eye on proceedings as Goody Petronelli and his son Tony tend to a cut I received fighting against Tony Thornton.
(PHOTO: JAMES HIGGINS)

ABOVE: The Collins clan invaded Boston to see my first world title fight against Mike McCallum. Here I am with my brothers Roddy, Paschal and Mick. BELOW: Despite being a little overawed at first, I came desperately close to taking McCallum's title away. No amount of money, he said, would convince him to give me a rematch. (PHOTO: JAMES MEEHAN / INPHO)

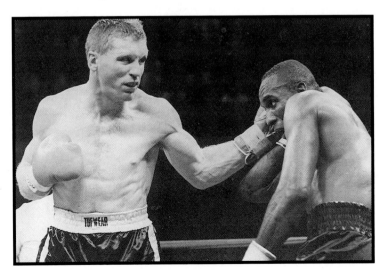

**Relaxing with my daughter Caoimhe and
son Stevie during our time in Boston.**

After returning to Ireland to resume my career, I found a new home at the Beresford guest house in Bangor. (PHOTO: BILLY STICKLAND / INPHO)

Barney Eastwood watches as I feel the strain during a sparring session in his world-famous gym in Belfast in 1991. (PHOTO: BILLY STICKLAND / INPHO)

ABOVE: **Another world title fight, another defeat; this time I come even closer to beating the Texan Reggie Johnson in New Jersey in 1992.** (PHOTO: ALAN BETSON / INPHO) BELOW: **Showing the scars of battle, I am left to contemplate my future after losing to Johnson.** (PHOTO: BILLY STICKLAND / INPHO)

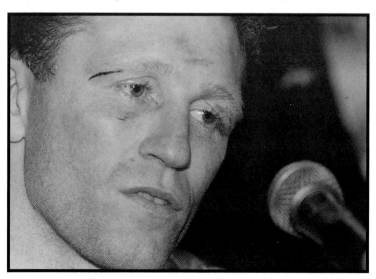

Third time lucky: Chris Pyatt crumbles in the fifth round as I finally go on to become a world champion. (PHOTO: JOHN GICHIGI / ALLSPORT)

**The Celtic Warrior is born: my lifetime ambition is achieved
as I show off the WBO middleweight title belt.**

Savouring the happiest moment of my life with my mother Colette and my wife Gemma on arrival back in Dublin after my victory over Pyatt, May 1994. (PHOTO: BILLY STICKLAND / INPHO)

The limousine swung into the carpark underneath the Ponds Forge, and I stepped out. Kitbag slung over my shoulder, I took the elevator to the first floor, got into the dressing-room and shut the door behind me. Those tortuous months of waiting, all the uncertainty, the lonely weeks away from my family in Romford, they were at an end now. Tonight was what it was all about. Taking off my sunglasses, cap and jacket, I went over to the mirror and started shadowboxing, as the room filled with voices behind me.

'Tonight's your night, Stevie,' I heard someone say.

'Do the job.'

'New champ.'

'You're the man, Steve, show him.'

I rummaged through my bag to check my equipment. Mouthpiece, shorts, boots, grease. I had everything. Prayer time. I asked God not that I would win, but that I would be given a fair chance, that Pyatt and I would compete on equal terms. Beyond the door, the clamour was beginning to rise. Naseem Hamed, a flashy twenty-year-old who called himself The Prince, was humiliating the European champion, Vincenzo Belcastro, and the crowd were loving it.

I thought about some of the people who were out there, friends who'd travelled the world to watch me box. I wondered what they were thinking. They knew that this was my last chance. I thought about my father. He would have been proud to see me here, to know that even after all the disappointments, I'd picked myself up again and come back. I knew that this was his dream, and had been from the very first day he strapped that headguard on me at Maxie McCullough's gym on Gardiner Street.

I pulled on my foul-protector, shorts and boots and one of Pyatt's men came in to watch my hands being bandaged. So many thoughts were flitting through my mind. Some of them were strange thoughts. I looked around at the dressing-room and thought how similar it was to every dressing-room I'd ever been in in my career, and I thought: Well, Steve, here you are again. And I looked around at the faces and everyone looked so forlorn, so lost in thought. I saw it in their eyes. They were thinking: God, please let this be his night.

When my hands were wrapped, I gave a nod to Pyatt's observer and hoped he'd go back and tell him how confident I seemed. An official from the British Boxing Board of Control brought in my gloves and the sight of them started my adrenalin flowing, as it always does. Out in the arena, the noise was deafening as Hamed showboated his way through the final round and took the European title. There was a rap on my dressing-room door and in walked a young, heavily made-up woman, wearing a *Daily Mirror* T-shirt, short skirt and high heels.

'What do you want?' someone asked her.

'Oh, I'm here to carry the Irish flag into the ring.'

'No way,' I said. 'I'm not having some dolly-bird carrying my flag.' With feelings beginning to run high, I was very rude to her. Never mind. I'd apologise later. But, as far as I was concerned, carrying the tricolour into the ring was an honour and one I'd always reserved for my closest friends. As she left, very much upset by my remark, I asked Silky to do it. He seemed so proud.

An official put his head around the door and told us it was time to go. I walked as far as the door and stopped. When I come back through here again, I thought, I'll either be champion of the world or a boxer about to announce his retirement. I let out a shout: 'YAH! Here we go,' and there were yells of encouragement from behind me. Hood up and head down, I walked up to the ring to the strains of 'Whiskey in the Jar' and I could feel people patting me on the back and voices I recognised wishing me luck.

I felt no tension once I stepped out of the dressing-room, no nerves or fears. Just a strange calm. That worried me and I hoped I'd feel more fired up when the fight started.

My gown looked about five sizes too big for me, with a large hood that covered my eyes. But I wanted it that way for a reason. Any parent who has a child who won't sleep at night without the bedroom light on will have explained to their son or daughter that what they're frightened of isn't the dark at all, they're frightened of what they can't see. Adults are scared of that too. So I planned to use this piece of amateur psychology on Pyatt, who wouldn't be allowed to see my face until the first bell sounded and I was in front of him.

When I got to the ring, I loosened up, while Pyatt made his way from his dressing-room. The moment I heard the music he'd chosen, I knew his mind was filled with doubts about this fight. It was that 'bad attitude' American rap music. I looked out from under the hood as he shuffled towards the ring, wearing no robe, grimacing, rolling his shoulders and flexing his neck muscles. Shit, I thought, he's trying to look like Mike Tyson. It just wasn't Pyatt's style. But if he thought he was going to strike fear into me with that music and that look, he was wrong. Far from being intimidated, I saw it as a sign of weakness.

Pushing the 'Britain *vs* Ireland' theme seemed to have done the trick for Frank Warren, I thought, as the crowd broke into a chorus of 'Rule Britannia'. As the emcee introduced us, Pyatt made several attempts to catch my eye, as his seconds massaged his shoulders and whispered encouragement in his ear, as though he were a prize pit-bull terrier being prepared for a fight. He was very keen to eyeball me when the referee called us to the centre of the ring to give us our instructions, but, even with the gown off, I kept my head down and still refused to make eye contact. I went back to the corner, the bell sounded, I blessed myself and turned around. We looked into each other's eyes for the first time. I don't know what he saw in mine, but in his I saw fear.

My only worry was that I was as calm when the first bell rang as I had been on the walk to the ring. That explains the tentative start to the fight. It was about twenty seconds before either of us threw a meaningful punch. I caught him with a couple of shots, but neither hurt him. The next punch I hit him with was a left, which didn't quite land cleanly and he dropped both his hands and mockingly fell back onto the ropes. I did manage to hit him cleanly on the forehead and he started to use a very unorthodox defensive style, bending right down, almost doubled over, so I had to punch downwards and found it difficult to hit him. I threw a combination of five punches, all of which he smothered on his gloves and forearms. He caught me with a shot as I came inside and he chased after me as I staggered backwards, losing my footing. As the bell rang, I was confident I'd won the round for my greater accuracy with my punches. Back in the corner, Freddy told me I was doing fine and told me to keep my jab going and to maybe try some hooks and the upper cut in the second.

Pyatt began the second more purposefully than he had the first, trying to force the pace of the fight, but he was still throwing his punches recklessly, and I caught him cold coming in with a right to the side of his head and followed it up with a left. He dropped a beautiful right on me, but again, hard though it was, it didn't hurt much, and it was one of the few punches he threw that I didn't see coming. His cornermen shouted: 'Work the body, Chris. Work the body.' It was obvious he was going to try to weaken my legs by winding me or bruising my ribs and sides. The best punches of the round, though, were thrown right on the bell, with him hitting me with a strong left hook, while I wobbled him with an even heavier shot. Again, I was confident that my greater precision had given me that round.

When I slipped and ended up on the canvas twice in the third round, many people felt I was losing my composure. The reverse was actually the case. I was too composed and my footwork was out of co-ordination because of it. The first time, my feet just disappeared from under me as I moved backwards. A few seconds later, I put all my body weight into a right hook, Pyatt saw it coming and ducked and I ended up on my back again. The crowd roared every time he landed a punch, even if it only cuffed me, and I hoped that that wouldn't influence the judges. He got through with a few hard shots in the third round as he upped the tempo. A right caught me cleanly and, as I backed onto the ropes, he hit me square on the nose with a shot that snapped my head backwards. I managed to get off the ropes, but he caught me an uppercut, which again jerked my head back and I nodded in aesthetic appreciation, as if to say: Good shot, Chris. He got through with a body shot too, burying a punch into my right hand rib-cage. The crowd were roaring 'Pyyyyy-at, Pyyyyy-at, Pyyyyy-at,' as I returned to the corner, still believing that, despite Pyatt's best round, I was still in control.

The most significant moment of the fight came in the opening seconds of the fourth round, when I walked across the ring and right onto the end of a thunderous right, which had all of Pyatt's weight behind it. THUMP! I moved my head back to ride the punch. When I regained my composure, I knew it was the best punch he was going to throw all night. And it hadn't hurt me. I knew that that was all he had. My confidence was fired. I started to notice Pyatt dropping his left hand, just as he had on the video tapes I'd watched and I felt it was only a matter of time until he did it long enough for me to send a punch over the top and knock him out. He must have known that I'd withstood his best shot, but he continued to look for the knockout. He reverted to the tactic of bending over, backing onto the ropes, trying to draw me in and get me to open up. He eventually came out and brought a beautiful right hook crashing across my face. I replied with two good shots of my own and he landed with one more before the round ended.

Seldom before had I ever felt in such complete control. I began the fifth round by landing a three-shot combination and I ducked as he swung out wildly. I connected with a very strong right and then we went into a clinch. 'Sort yourselves out,' the referee said, and we pulled back from each other. I watched eagerly as Pyatt prepared to throw another wild right and I wondered whether he'd drop his left again. When it came, the punch missed by inches and, yes, the left went down. In an instant, I hit him square in the face with a right that came from my shoulder. His eyes became vacant and I could see that he was about to fall forward onto me. So I spun around and he turned as he fell, landing on his back, his feet going almost back over his head as he hit the canvas.

His eyes looked glassy when he climbed to his feet again. He was badly hurt. As the referee picked up the count, Pyatt almost fell forward onto him. His legs were shot. We were waved on and Pyatt widened his stance to stop himself falling over. He fell back onto the ropes and I moved in to finish him off. I rained punches down on him, but he fought back gamely, throwing an uppercut that narrowly missed my chin. I threw every punch I knew at him. I felt the impact on my knuckles and could hear the thud as I hit his head. He made two more attempts to get out of trouble, catching me once with a left hook. But he was too weak to get off the ropes. He swung from side to side, desperately trying to avoid punishment and I eased up and started throwing my punches more deliberately. Blood had started to flow from his nose. Jimmy Tibbs screamed from his corner: 'Go down, Chris. Go down.' It isn't in the nature of most fighters to go down voluntarily, but it would have bought Pyatt another ten seconds in which to recover and got closer to the end of the round. But he couldn't go down, because he didn't have any flexibility in his legs anymore. His knees wouldn't bend. Eventually the referee stepped in between us and waved it all over.

Pyatt trudged back to his corner, while I stepped backwards, struggling to take it in, as bodies started hurtling through the ropes towards me. The first person I saw was Roddy, who must have been in before the fight was over. How the rest managed to get through the cordon of bouncers around the ring only they can explain, particularly my uncle Terry, who'd had a triple heart bypass operation a few years before. I saw Paschal literally standing on people's heads and shoulders to get through, until two security guards caught a leg each and tried to drag him out just as he was ducking under the ropes. But his left leg was between the top and middle ropes and his right was between the middle and bottom, so there he was, howling in agony as his balls were being crushed by the rope. He somehow kicked free, and the ring was so completely swamped with people they didn't bother chasing after him.

Meanwhile, I was having what I could only describe as an out-of-body experience, a phenomenon I was sceptical about until that night. My brother Mick and Johnny Kenna, an old friend of ours from Cabra, were lifting me up. Everyone around me was screaming and crying. I couldn't hear them. I felt like I was watching it all from the other side of the ring. And everything was happening in slow motion. I felt so at ease. It was the strangest few minutes I'd ever known. I felt as though my father was in the ring with me. I knew this had been Dad's dream as much as mine and, though I've never really come to terms with his death and know that I can never bring him back, for those few minutes I thought I had. There was a huge weight of expectation being lifted from my shoulders. It felt physical.

Even during those depressing months in Romford, when I thought I realised what being a world champion meant to me, I didn't at all. I didn't appreciate just how much I'd allowed it to take over my life or how everything was forced to play second fiddle to my obsession. Even my wife and children. I was looking at Gemma and my mother, Colette, seeing how happy they were that I'd got what I wanted. It didn't matter what happened after tonight. Even if I died the next day or if I got knocked out by the first punch in my very next fight, I had won a world title and no-one could ever take that away from me.

Barry Hearn told me that ITV's Gary Newbon wanted to interview me live on television. He held open the ropes, I climbed out and sat on the side of the ring. 'It was some punch to win a championship,' Newbon began. 'It's the third attempt by you to win a world title and now you've done it.'

So many different thoughts were careering around in my mind, I didn't know quite how to start. 'It seems the only way I'm going to win big fights is by knockout,' I said, 'because I know I beat Reggie Johnson and I know I took Mike McCallum all the way to the wire and some people thought I'd done it. It's been hard getting there. I've worked hard. I had my first fight twenty-one years ago. And my dedication to being world champion ... I feel like crying I'm so happy ... I wanna dedicate ...'

Gary Newbon interrupted. 'Let me show you this knockdown,' he said. So I put my glove in front of the camera. 'Let me say something. I dedicate that fight to the best middleweight in the world, my late father, Paschal Collins.'

CHAPTER 5

World Champion

WILD NIGHT IN SHEFFIELD

Pyatt and I made our way back to our dressing-rooms after the fight. Mine was deserted except for Barry Hearn, who was standing just inside the door, and a stranger in a suit. 'Steve, don't get mad,' said Barry. 'This guy has something to give you.' The man handed me what he explained was a writ on behalf of the Petronellis, who were, it seemed, now determined to try to have the judgement against me registered in Britain. Suddenly, as a world champion, my earning capacity had gone up and they obviously wanted a piece of the action. How much money was this guy being given to serve me this writ, I wondered. How much was he being paid to spoil the biggest night of my life? Maybe £30 or £40? Apparently, he'd made several attempts to serve me with the piece of paper before the fight, but Barry persuaded him to hold off until I got back to the dressing-room, worried that I might enter the ring in a fragile state of mind if I knew about it beforehand. As I looked at this piece of paper and this man in a suit in front of me, all I knew was that if Barry walked out of the room at that moment and left me alone with this man I might not be able to resist the urge to hit him or throw the slops bucket over his head. But I wasn't going to let him ruin my night, so I simply called him an asshole and he left in a bit of a hurry.

Barry told me not to worry, that things would be sorted out. The writ didn't particularly bother me, though. I didn't see any way that, if I put my case in a British court, as I would this time, a judge could say that my appearance at a press conference for a fight that never happened was worth $250,000 to my former managers. No, this wasn't a night for worries anyway.

Within a few minutes, the dressing-room had become just one big, heaving mass of bodies, singing, crying and dancing all at once. We were all roaring drunkenly, but the only intoxicating substance any of us had had was the emotion of the occasion. Everyone wanted to buckle the belt around his waist and to tell me that he felt as though he'd won it himself. That's how much these people lived my dream. Barry Hearn and Freddy King danced around like a couple of excited schoolchildren. There's a photograph of the two of them in the ring after the fight. Barry has his mouth open and he's grabbing Freddy and Freddy looks like a kid about to cry. I hoped Barry would take the photograph of Pyatt down from his wall and replace it with this one. Freddy said it was the most satisfying day of his career as a trainer, because he knew what I'd suffered in the months beforehand – the setbacks, the depression, the politics, the gamesmanship. And because he worked so close to me, he felt as though he'd lived it himself. Barry said he'd listened so many times to Freddy telling him that I was going to beat Pyatt, but thought it was nothing more than wishful thinking.

Tony Griffiths, a raw, tough sparring partner I'd worked with in the weeks before the fight, was very excited at the thought that, every afternoon over the last few weeks, he'd been on the end of the same punch that put Pyatt down, but had managed to stand up to all of them himself. 'You beat him with exactly the same punch you've been throwing at me,' he said. 'I feel like I'm really part of winning this title.'

The party was already well under way by the time I got back to the hotel. Fifty or sixty of us sang, talked, told jokes and reminisced through the night and into the next morning. There were people there I'd known since I was a child. There were others who didn't even know my name at the start of the night. One group of lads had come from Birmingham to see one of the fights on the undercard, were persuaded to come back to the hotel and, just before they stretched out on the sofas and went to sleep at 5am, were talking about coming back to Ireland with us to carry on the party in Dublin. My chauffeur, who didn't drink, also came in and, by the end of the night, said he felt like an honorary Irishman.

Everyone had a story to tell. One of my favourites involved Johnny Kenna, a lad we grew up with in Cabra who now worked as a cobbler in Manchester. A nicer lad you couldn't meet. Johnny was blessed with two very special gifts when he was born – a brass neck and the gift of the gab. Unable to get a ticket for the fight, he was not to be discouraged. He put on his tuxedo and made his way to the Ponds Forge, where he spotted Frank Warren getting out of a limousine in the carpark. Quick as a flash, Johnny was over to the door, stood in front of him, looked long and hard at him and said: 'Oh, Frank, you're all right, go on in.' Seeing the suit and the way he checked Warren's credentials, the doormen presumed Johnny was one of them. He started to check people's tickets at the door, and the doormen didn't feel they needed to ask any questions when he said: 'Right lads, I'm just nipping inside here for a cup of coffee. Watch the fort for us, will yiz?' And in he walked. Oh, and he didn't settle for a cheap bucket seat at the back either. Johnny sat ringside for the entire fight!

Roddy talked excitedly about the interview he'd done with a local television station that afternoon. Apparently, as he and a group of friends left the hotel on the way down to a local pub, he saw a TV news crew in the carpark opposite. Roddy was dressed very casually, while the other lads, who were all wearing black suits, looked like minders for somebody very famous. So the crew, believing Roddy to be 'someone', called him over. 'Do you want to do the interview here?' said Roddy, without the slightest hint of a smile.

'Well, who are you?' the reporter asked nervously.

'Roddy Collins, Republic of Ireland international and brother of boxer Stephen Collins.'

Now only half of that statement was true, of course, but the interviewer was prepared to give him the benefit of the doubt. He said they were conducting a vox-pop of opinions about Naseem Hamed, the bantamweight boxer who was fighting on the undercard. I don't think Roddy had ever heard of him, but, not willing to let that spoil his moment of fame, he managed to talk knowlegeably about him for a full five minutes. We never found out whether it made the news that day, but Roddy felt he'd put on such a good performance that it had to have.

At 5am I went to bed, but was too excited to sleep and, an hour and a half later, was up again, enjoying breakfast with Silky and my new friends from Sheffield's black and Asian communities. Because I had some business to take care of back in Romford, I didn't plan to return to Dublin until the following day. But I got some inkling as to how serious my achievement was being taken back in Ireland when a researcher from 'The Gay Byrne Show' phoned and asked whether I'd be prepared to do an interview live on the radio with Gay himself. I jumped at the opportunity.

The first chance I had to see the fight was on the drive back to London. The limousine was fitted with a television and video and, as we left Sheffield and headed south, Aidan Cooney of 98FM, his girlfriend Audrey, Gemma and I sat glued to it, reliving every moment of it. And then reliving it some more. The rewind button on the remote control was working overtime.

Before we left Sheffield, I phoned ahead to the Matchroom office and asked them to book a party for about twenty or thirty people at Secret's Nightclub in Romford that night. When we arrived at the Matchroom 'villa', we rounded up a group of friends who lived locally. This was to be my night. There was a forewarning for them all, that if anyone put his hand in his pocket to try to pay for anything, they would be thrown out.

A couple of hours before the party started, I got a call from an old man who lives in London's East End and who used to hang around the gym quite a bit. I'd always wondered about him, about his background especially. He had all the credentials of a street-wise operator – the husky voice, the cockney accent, the way he'd talk to you in a hushed tone.

Whatever he'd done, I liked him. He was one of London's old stock, and he loved boxing. And he took a particular shine to me.

'Ow roight, Steve, well done, mate,' he said on the phone.

'Thanks.'

'Where ya goin' tonight, mate, Secrets?'

'Yeh ...'

'Right, we'll be daan.'

His arrival was a sight to behold. He walked in with four or five of his friends, all wearing long, black coats over the best-fitting suits. One by one, they hugged me and kissed me on the cheeks until I felt as though my name was Colleoni and not Collins, and these people were the London mob, who were thanking me for taking a dive so they could collect big from the bookies.

While I didn't have the courage to ask him straight out about his shadowy past, the curiosity was killing me. It got worse later in the evening, when we went to a local restaurant. Everyone recognised him and his friends there and spoke to them reverently. We didn't even have to pay for our meals. Whoever these men were, they commanded a very deep respect. But what did they do? I wanted to know badly. Gemma spared me the embarrassment of having to ask, when she said, in all innocence: 'So, lads, what do you all do for a living?'

Silence. I shuddered as I watched them look at each other, then at Gemma and me, then back at each other again. And then they all broke into a fit of hysterics. When it had died down, one of them said: 'Ah, ya know, luv, this and that.' The laughter began again.

DUBLIN CAN BE HEAVEN

While the fact that Gay Byrne wanted to talk me gave me some idea of how seriously RTE were taking me, I didn't know quite how the country was reacting as I boarded the flight home. I was the first Dubliner to win a world boxing title. But I also considered myself the first *true* Irishman to win one, because none of the other thirteen Irish fighters who won world titles had carried both an Irish boxing licence and an Irish passport like I did.

After the plane touched down and was steered towards the terminal building, I could see the dignitaries lining up to meet me and was told that Dublin's Lord Mayor, Tomás MacGiolla, was among them. When the plane lumbered to a halt, I was ushered up to the top door and, when it opened, I held the belt aloft for the RTE camera crew. By the time I got to the bottom of the steps, there was a huge surge of bodies towards me – my mum, my brothers and sisters, uncles, neighbours, friends and the few well-wishers who'd managed to get through security and out onto the runway. Through this huge mass of people, I noticed Gemma walking out with Clodagh, our baby, in her arms, and Stevie and Caoimhe beside her. The two older children ran towards me and I gathered them up in my arms. I didn't want to let them go. Clodagh had changed so much in the weeks since I'd last seen her. I realised how much I'd been missing while I was away and this selfish thought came over me that I didn't want to be here at all, sharing this with everyone. I wanted to be somewhere else, just me, Gemma and the children, enjoying ourselves after all the sacrifices we'd made.

Tomás McGiolla came out to meet me, but, with Stevie sitting on one arm and Caoimhe on the other, I couldn't shake his hand, so he clasped me by the shoulders and told me I'd done Dublin proud. A press conference had been arranged in the Aer Rianta hospitality room. Inside, it was bedlam. There must have been a hundred or more people crammed into this small room, standing on tables and chairs, taking up whatever vantage points they could to get a glimpse of the table at the top of the room, where I was sitting with Gemma and the children. The television lights were blinding as I answered questions from every angle and looked around, picking out the people I recognised in this huge collage of faces in front of me, still trying to take it all in. And everything I said was punctuated by this loud 'Yeh!' from the crowd.

'My life is complete now. I've got my family and my world title and I couldn't ask for more.'

'*Yeeehhh!*'

'I'm the first true Irish world champion in boxing, because I'm the first Irishman with a green passport and an Irish boxing licence to do it.'

'*Yeeehhh!*'

'Every time I fought, I represented my country. I believe I showed the true fighting qualities of the Irish. I never gave up. I don't believe I ever let myself, my fans or my country down.'

'*Yeeehhh!*'

After the press conference, I picked the children up again and we were shepherded back across the tarmac, into the terminal building and through the Arrivals gate, where several hundred people were waiting to greet me. After half an hour or so, we finally reached the sanctuary of the car that a good friend, Michael Fitzsimons of DG Opel fame, had given us for the drive back to Cabra, where a street party was being held. The drive to Annamoe Terrace was an experience I'll never forget. Flags and bunting hung from every lamppost, every window. Banners saying: 'Cabra's pride' and 'Steve Collins – we love you.' Michael wound open the sunroof to allow me to stand up in the back and show off the belt through the roof. Guinness had sent five hundred cans of stout and beer down to the house – an admission perhaps that all those mornings the company's biggest skiver had spent in the Phoenix Park and the swimming pool when he should have been working had been worth it after all. Neighbours who, twenty-five years earlier, used to knock on our door to tell my mother that I'd run through their gardens or had broken their windows with a ball, were all hugging me now and telling me how proud they were of me.

Early in the evening, a researcher from the 'Late Late Show' phoned and asked whether I'd be prepared to appear on the show that night. The Late Late Show? I thought. Finally, I've made it! Also, a recording of the show is broadcast on Channel Four and I was eager to boost my profile in Britain now that I was a world champion. It was a great opportunity and I jumped at the chance.

With so many people phoning and wanting to meet me, we decided that the house we were renting on the Navan Road just wasn't big enough for entertaining – in fact, it was hardly big enough for Gemma and the children to live in. So we decided to check into the Burlington hotel, where the manager put us up in a luxury suite.

THE PRICE OF FAME!

That night, I was sitting with my friend the comedian Brendan O'Carroll, enjoying a couple of pints, when I thought I recognised a face on the other side of the hotel bar. 'Is that Paul McStay, the Celtic player?' I wondered.

Having been out of the country for most of the year, I'd forgotten that the FAI Cup final was on at Lansdowne Road the next day. And Sligo Rovers, an unfashionable First Division side, had pulled off the unthinkable and won a place in the final against Derry City. Sligo were managed at the time by Willie McStay, Paul's brother. Paul was a hero of mine and I was dying to meet him.

By this time, McStay had noticed that we were talking about him and he was staring back at us. And then he walked over.

'Steve Collins?' he said. 'I'm really sorry for interrupting you here, but I just wanted to introduce myself.'

I was absolutely delighted. 'What are you apologising for?' I asked. 'I've been dying to go over and talk to you, but I didn't have the guts. I didn't know whether you'd know who I was.'

'Are you kidding?' he said. 'When you beat Chris Pyatt, you don't know how proud you made us feel in Glasgow. Especially wearing the tartan and the Celtic Warrior on your shorts.'

It was such a thrill. Paul McStay. A hero of mine – and he knew who I was. He'd watched me beat Pyatt. I'd made him feel proud! We went to meet his friends who'd travelled over from Glasgow for the match. Sitting amongst them was another familiar face – Alan McManus, the snooker player.

'Here, Alan! Do you know who this is?' Paul asked him.

He looked up at me. 'Ah yeh, I know who that is,' he said after a pause. 'It's that taxi driver who was slagging me earlier on, isn't it?' We laughed so much, we almost had to go out for air.

I was a little bit disappointed at the civic reception that was hosted in my honour at the Mansion House. The gesture was a very good one, it's just that it was too ... well, small. I was told by the woman from Dublin Corporation that the number of people I could invite was limited to forty. That meant that a lot of people who'd followed my career from my earliest amateur days were disappointed. There were people I wanted there, like members of the Irish Ex-Boxers Association and a few more officials from the Irish Amateur Boxing Association. One woman from the IABA actually phoned my house to ask rather bluntly whether they'd done anything to offend me, because so few of them had been asked. A lot of people were left with their noses out of joint and, while it was supposed to be one of the proudest days of my life, I spent weeks afterwards apologising to people and having to make explanations.

After the 'Late Late Show' appearance I couldn't walk down Henry Street without being recognised. Dublin people aren't like the Americans. They're much more stand-offish. In Boston, they'd interrupt your conversation to get your autograph and, even though I've never begrudged signing them, there's much more respect for your privacy back home. Usually, people just look at you, and then look at you again, but don't come over to talk or ask for your signature until someone else gets the courage to do it first. I'd be sitting in Bewley's on Grafton Street and notice people staring at me, but they wouldn't know they were staring. Suddenly, I had this public persona in Dublin that I'd never had before and I had to watch my Ps and Qs. But I liked it.

Still, it has its disadvantages too. Standing in a bar, you can become a beacon for every drunk who has enough Dutch courage on him to shape up to you to try to impress his mates. I had one particular experience in June in a bar in New York, where I was celebrating Ireland's victory over Italy in the World Cup with a few friends. I'd actually flown first to Las Vegas to watch Roberto Duran lose to Vinnie Pazienza, who was still being touted as a possible future opponent for me. But, after getting my hands on a ticket for the match, I booked a flight for New York. Sadly, the flight was delayed and Ray Houghton was just putting the ball in the Italian net as we touched down at JFK. So I headed straight for Doran's bar, where I knew the atmosphere would be great. And it was. Until some idiot walked up beside me, said: 'Ahh, Collins,' and punched me on the top of my arm. Now, it wasn't a playful dig at all. He obviously fancied himself as a fighter and this was designed to show his friends what a bit of a lad he was. And he'd go back to wherever he was from in Ireland with the story that he'd hit Steve Collins a box in a bar in New York. So I wasn't going to let him away with it. I turned around and glared at him. 'Don't ever try that again,' I said. Sensing that I was serious, he turned around and kept a low profile for the rest of the night.

There were days when I liked going back to being just plain old Steve and enjoying a pint with a few mates. One evening stands out for me. Brendan O'Carroll talked me into going to see Tottenham play against Shelbourne at Tolka Park. Jurgen Klinsmann had signed for Spurs after the World Cup, thus the excitement about the game. But Shelbourne made them look very ordinary that night. Afterwards, we teamed up with Aidan Cooney from 98FM radio and the then Shelbourne manager Eamonn Gregg for a few pints. The night finished with a visit to a takeaway and I have this memory of the four of us, standing in a shop doorway on Dorset Street, drunk as skunks, stuffing ourselves with kebabs at one o'clock in the morning. It was nice to be ... well, normal again. After the summer I'd had, it was good to forget about my public image for the night. Perhaps Brendan O'Carroll liked to forget that he was one of Ireland's leading comedians, Eamonn Gregg that he was manager of the richest club in the League of Ireland and Aidan Cooney that he had to be up early the next morning to read the sports news to tens of thousands of Dubliners.

BACK TO SERIOUS BUSINESS

My attitude towards boxing changed after what happened in Sheffield. All I'd ever wanted from it was a world title and now that my ambition was fulfilled, I owed it to my family to build a secure future for them before somebody took it from me. I had the potential to earn a lot of money in the United States, where I was already very well known. But what happened back in the dressing-room at the Ponds Forge had brought my problems with the Petronellis into sharper focus. It had to be sorted out. They knew that to get the judgement against me in Britain, the facts of the case would have to be debated in open court, because I was going to contest it this time. If they lost the case in Britain, then I'd have very good reason to go back to the United States try to and have that judgement overturned on appeal. The issuing of the writ that night in Sheffield was intended to remind me that, regardless of whether I won or not that night, I would never earn as much money as I should from boxing until I paid them $250,000.

I phoned Pat Petronelli at his home in Boston on 10 August and laid my cards on the table. It was futile making demands on me like that, I told him, because I simply didn't have the money. The only way I could earn that kind of money was to return to America to fight. If I did that, I suggested, we might be able to come to an arrangement whereby he'd be involved in the promotion of my fights along with Barry Hearn and he'd collect a percentage of each purse until it reached an agreed figure. He seemed to be on the point of accepting it, and eventually he said he'd talk to his legal people and call me back a few days later. He didn't. It was around this time that I approached Henri Brandman, a London-based solicitor whose clients include George Michael and Frank Bruno, and asked him to put together my defence.

A week later, the prospect of returning to America to fight was put to the back of my mind. The Mole phoned me at home and said he wanted to meet me to discuss an offer that Frank Warren and Barney Eastwood wanted to make me. Because he knew me well, he'd been asked to act as an intermediary. On paper the deal was an exciting one, primarily because it involved a fight in Dublin. He said I'd be given £100,000 to fight a middleweight from Leicester called Shawn Cummins or 'a suitable opponent', and if I won, a further £120,000 to fight Belfast's Ray Close, who for the second time in a year had come close to beating Chris Eubank. Both fights would take place before the end of the year with Warren and Eastwood promoting the fights jointly. I said I was interested and that I'd discuss it with my manager, Barry Hearn, but I said I wanted the offer in writing before I agreed to anything. I'm glad I asked for it. When The Mole rang a couple of days later, the offer had changed slightly. Instead of getting £100,000 for the Cummins fight, the offer was now £80,000 plus £20,000 worth of tickets for the show, which I would have to sell myself. And instead of £120,000 for Close I'd get £100,000 and £20,000 worth of tickets. It's not an uncommon method of paying fighters, but I didn't want the hassle of having to find someone who could shift the tickets. So I said that I was happy with the deal he had proposed originally and would accept nothing less. I arranged to meet him that Friday, 19 August in, of all places, the carpark at McDonald's in Phibsboro. Just how sinister this appeared was not exactly lost on me as we sat in the back of the car handling documents for a deal worth a quarter of a million pounds! He handed me a draft of the contract which I faxed on to Hearn.

Sky Sports television asked me to commentate on Chris Eubank's fight with Sammy Storey in Cardiff and the job gave me the opportunity to meet up with Eastwood who was in Wales for the fight. My relationship with Warren had been difficult to say the least, but he knew that Eastwood and I were friends and seemed content to let him conduct the negotiations on their behalf. We talked about the deal and I got very excited, especially about the prospect of fighting in Dublin. The following Monday, 29 August, I phoned Eastwood at home to tell him I wanted a few minor amendments made to the contract and he said that he didn't foresee any problems about them. Two days later, I left for London to start training for the fight. I was glad to get back into training because, after the summer I'd had, I felt fat and out of shape. I began enthusiastically in the gym, aiming to get my weight right down again.

The excitement lasted less than twenty-four hours. Frank Warren faxed his version of the contract to Hearn's office and it was completely different to the one we'd discussed with Eastwood. It was hazy, involved less money, different fighters, obscure promises of other fights – probably this guy and probably that. I was gutted. I have a great deal of respect for Barney Eastwood. He's very proud to be an Irishman and has done a huge service to boxing. When he was my manager, he staged my fight against Danny Morgan at the National Stadium in 1991 and I think he was genuinely excited about doing the same thing again.

I felt that my Achilles' heel had been exposed: I would agree to practically anything just to get the opportunity to fight in Dublin again. Too many people in the sport knew it. After this, I went to Hearn and told him to send faxes to every fight promoter and manager in Britain to tell them not to contact me with fight offers. They would all have to go through him instead. He had the stomach for fight negotiations. They just broke my heart.

CHAPTER 6

High Farce in Hong Kong

The entire summer of 1994 had passed and I hadn't brought home a paypacket and, after the collapse of plans for my fight in Dublin, I didn't know what I was going to do next. But then a new opportunity presented itself.

'High Noon in Hong Kong' was the brainchild of John Daly, a California-based Londoner, whose company, Hemdale Communications Inc, had been involved in financing Oscar-winning films like *Platoon* and *The Last Emperor*. Daly had had only one previous involvement in boxing, but it was enough to convince some of the sport's top promoters that his second venture could be just as successful. Back in 1974, he co-promoted the famous 'Rumble in the Jungle' fight between Muhammad Ali and George Foreman in Kinshasa, Zaire. While staging a boxing show in Hong Kong was seen as ambitious, putting one on in Zaire had been considered outrageous in the 1970s. Okay, back then, Daly did have the help of a young, jive-talking fledgling promoter, Don King.

The arrangement between the two for the Zaire show had been quite simple. Daly provided the front-money and King provided ... well, the front. He had had the audacity to approach Foreman, who was the heavyweight champion of the world, and ask whether he'd be prepared to defend his title against Ali for $5m, a figure that was unprecedented for a fight back then. Foreman agreed and King approached Ali's manager, Herbert Muhammad, with a similar offer, which was also accepted. Armed with Daly's front-money, King set off for Zaire, one of Africa's newest countries, talked his way into an audience with President Mobutu Sese Seko and persuaded him to part with the $10m dollars he needed. In return, when the fight was staged, King told him, one billion television viewers would focus on Kinshasa on the night of the fight and Mobutu's name and that of Zaire would be spread across the earth. The rest, as they say, is history.

King wasn't involved this time, but Bob Arum, his arch rival, was, and everyone figured some of King's magic was bound to have rubbed off on Daly when they co-promoted the Rumble. 'High Noon in Hong Kong' involved much the same principle – bringing a very expensive and high-profile boxing show to a country which, in the past, had shown practically no interest in the sport. Despite its population of six million people, Hong Kong had only fifteen boxing clubs (by comparison, in Ireland there are 274). But the sport had caught on in other Far East countries, especially Japan, Thailand and South Korea, all of which had world champions in the lighter weight divisions. So why not Hong Kong? After all, it did have a reputation for hosting top-class international sports events.

Hearn was well aware of this. He'd already done for snooker what Daly was attempting to do for boxing, having been at the forefront of the great snooker boom in the Far East in the 1980s. He led his Matchroom team of Steve Davis, Terry Griffiths, Dennis Taylor and Tony Meo on a tour of Hong Kong, China and the New Territories. The EJ Riley snooker table company, in which he and Davis had a substantial shareholding, sold thousands of snooker tables on the back of it. Hearn may have been a little bit sceptical about the boxing show, but because his own genius was for making the inconceivable conceivable, he decided that Daly should be offered the benefit of the doubt and he agreed to put up WBO heavyweight champion Herbie Hide as the star attraction.

Daly's plan was to stage a United States versus Great Britain show, a 'Battle for World Supremacy', the venue being the spectacular 40,000-

seat, outdoor Hong Kong Stadium on Hong Kong Island. It would feature four fights. At the top of the bill, Hide would defend his title against Tommy Morrisson, a heavyweight from Arkansas, who had progressed from taking part in the famous Midwest Tough Man competitions to become the Great White Hope of his generation. Then there was the young Luton lightweight, Billy Schwer, whose father came from Kildare. He would challenge the wiry but powerful Mexican, Rafael Ruelas, for the IBF lightweight title. And, after losing his last world title fight to Lennox Lewis, Frank Bruno would make his comeback against the former Olympic gold medallist and former WBO world champion Ray Mercer. The fourth fight scheduled was to be between the British and Commonwealth champion Ross Hale and WBO light-welterweight champion Zack Padilla. But when Padilla collapsed during sparring and was discovered to have a small clot on his brain, they needed to find a replacement quickly, and preferably one with a world title. Hearn knew just the man.

When he told me about the show, I was very enthusiastic. As well as giving me a much-needed payday, 'High Noon in Hong Kong' would give me the opportunity to see a place I probably would never have visited, to experience another culture for a few weeks, and I was excited about going there as a world champion. It was about a week before my opponent was named. It was to be Lonny Beasley, a twenty-nine-year-old security guard from Detroit. The name was immediately familiar to me and I remembered watching him fight a few months earlier against Julio Cesar Green for the North American Boxing Federation light middle-weight title. It was a gruelling fight, with both men almost out on their feet as they stepped out for the twelfth and final round. One judge had Green ahead. The other two had Beasley in front. Then came what must rank as one of the most farcical endings to a boxing match ever. Absolutely exhausted, Beasley tried to take a breather by going into a clinch, resting his chin on Green's shoulder and holding on to him for a few seconds. The referee prised the two of them apart, giving a firm shove to Beasley, who slumped backwards on to the canvas like a sack of potatoes and hadn't the strength to lift himself up again. I couldn't believe what I was seeing as the referee stood over him and counted him out, much to the annoyance of Augtin Sinegal, one of Beasley's cornermen, who chased the ref around the ring and then had to be ejected from Caesar's Palace to stop him hurting him.

While this fight was, for me, his most memorable, Beasley couldn't be taken lightly. He'd won fourteen of his first fifteen professional fights, though his progress was interrupted by a stint in the US army. Nonetheless, his record – 23 wins, 2 draws and 2 defeats – contained some very impressive wins. There was the victory against Charles Brewer, who was ranked sixth in the world by the IBF until Beasley confounded everyone, not least himself, by coming in as a last-minute replacement to knock him out in the first round. There was the win against another prospect, Emmet Linton, and the win and a draw he'd earned from his two fights with the hard-hitting Tony Marshall.

Despite his record, I wasn't really that concerned about him. He had fought for most of his career at junior middleweight, where he was never regarded as a hard puncher. At the heavier middleweight limit, he shouldn't have any chance of hurting me – as long as I kept my concentration.

Keeping my mind focused on the fight started to become difficult when the rumours began to circulate that the show was in trouble. Daly's dire cashflow problems were becoming evident in well-publicised rows with Wembley International, who owned the Hong Kong Stadium; the Regal Hong Kong hotel complained that five hundred rooms had been booked but not paid for; and the local boxing association hadn't received their sanctioning fee for the event. Despite numerous requests, Hearn had still not received the letters of credit which would guarantee our money for the show, and said that unless he did, neither Hide nor I would be travelling to Hong Kong. Daly's gamble was starting to look more than a little over-ambitious. He had managed to borrow $800,000 from the banks to help float the project in the first place, raising the cash against the anticipated income from the sale of tickets and subscriptions to

American pay-per-view television, both of which were now proving disappointing. This time, there was no President Mobutu Sese Seko to underwrite the show. Perhaps he should go to the Governor of Hong Kong, the former Tory party chairman Chris Patten, and try to tap him for $10m!

But the way I figured it, one of the wealthiest and most successful figures in the sport, Bob Arum, had lent his name to the promotion and, while he was involved, there was no way it was just going to fall apart. And anyway, as Harry Mullan, the editor of *Boxing News* put it, we all believed Daly would duck and dive in the great tradition of his namesake Arthur, and come midday on 23 October all of his current cashflow problems would just seem like a minor blip.

PUBLIC PERSONA

Against this uncertainty, it was difficult to find the motivation to resume training in the middle of September. I just had to convince myself that sorting out the financial problems was someone else's concern. My job was to be fit and to get my weight back down by the time I stepped on the scales on 22 October. Daly, Arum, Hearn, letters of credit and unpaid hotel bills all had to be shifted to the back of my mind.

Then I was given a bit of news that really annoyed me. To train for the fight, I'd have to leave the set-up in Romford and move fifty miles north to Norwich. Herbie Hide insisted on training in his home town and, because we shared the same trainer, Freddy King and I had to head north and work our own plans around his. Freddy didn't complain, but I resented it. The Matchroom gym was in Romford. Yet Hide, who was just twenty-three years old and held the same version of a world title as I did, was able to dictate where I trained for my first defence. Everybody in boxing panders to the heavyweights. For some reason, that I still don't understand, they exert this incredible fascination that fighters at other weights don't. And they command much greater purses for it too. Hide, for instance, was collecting over $1m for defending his WBO heavy-weight title, while I would be getting just $50,000 for putting my WBO middleweight title on the line.

Regardless of how wealthy and famous I become, I decided right from the start, I'll never allow myself to become so precious that I expect people to drop everything to fit around me and my plans. Whether there was a world title belt buckled around my waist or not, one of my biggest ambitions was always to remain the same down-to-earth Steve Collins who worked as an electrician at Guinness's brewery before he went off to America to chase his dream. Being recognised by complete strangers every time I go out is a bit of a thrill, I can't deny it, and I know there are millionaires who would give up everything they own just to have that kind of status and respect. Many have told me so. But I'll never let myself become a *prima donna* and that, as far as I'm concerned, is the mark of a truly great sportsman.

After a boxing show in Massachusetts a few years ago, I noticed Floyd Patterson, the former world heavyweight champion, patiently signing autographs for a crowd of about fifty or sixty people. On the table in front of him he had a stack of cards, each featuring his photograph and a printed signature. Now, it would have been the easiest thing in the world for him just to hand them out to the people and, because it was long past midnight, it would have been quite understandable too. But he didn't. He sat there, for what must have been forty-five minutes or more, asking people their names and writing personal messages. I remember thinking: 'That man has class.' If ever I become famous enough to attract a crowd of that size, I told myself, I'll handle it just as he did.

Just after I beat Pyatt, I got the opportunity. After being asked to join the footballer Niall Quinn as a guest of honour at the Blanchardstown Festival, one of our duties was to sign autographs. There were hundreds of children there and I'll never forget their faces. They were staring up at us, mouths and eyes opened wide in awe. I knew what it might mean to them in ten years' time to be able to say that I spoke nicely to them, let them hold my title belt and put my personal signature on one of the publicity cards that DG Opel had printed for me.

I made the most of the situation in Norwich. The training facilities, as it turned out, were first class. An enormous blue-and-white striped canopy was erected at the Barnham Broom Hotel and Leisure Centre and, for the following three weeks, that was where we went through the daily monotony of working the bags, lifting weights, skipping rope and sparring. We worked and lived in total seclusion, ten miles away from the nearest shop, with nothing to see but trees, fields, birds and horses. At times it bored us silly, but having no distractions helped.

A few days before we left for Hong Kong, Sky Television asked me to go to the studio in Hounslow to do another boxing analysis. I agreed. Then I remembered that I hadn't brought a suit to Norwich with me. So I went off and bought myself a very neatly-cut two-piece suit, which I discovered afterwards was very similar to the kind Chris Eubank wears (though probably several thousand pounds cheaper!). The lads in Norwich, who had sat glued to Sky Sports that evening, were waiting for me when I returned.

'Who the fuck do you think you are, Chris Eubank or something?' they teased.

'No, honestly, lads,' I protested. 'It was just coincidental. I didn't know he wore ...'

'Get out of it. You're trying to look like him, aren't you?'

Well, not quite. I did like the suit, but I'd draw the line at jodhpurs, riding boots, monocle and cane.

UNWELCOME PUBLICITY

About the same time, I received a telephone call from a journalist at *The Daily Sport* who said he was writing a preview piece about the show and asked whether I had a few minutes to talk to him. Now, for those not completely au fait with *The Daily Sport*, let's just say that it's not the kind of sports publication that its title suggests. Whatever coverage they give to boxing, soccer and snooker is usually squeezed in somewhere between sleazy photographs of women covering their private parts with a football or a cricket bat. Not my cup of tea. But, much to my subsequent regret, I agreed to talk to him.

'What are your plans after the Hong Kong fight, Steve? Will you move up a weight and take on some of the bigger names, maybe Chris Eubank, Roy Jones, James Toney?'

'Well,' I said, 'my priority is to earn as much money as I can for my family's future before I lose the title and I'm not going to go rushing into a very risky defence straight away.'

The 'preview' of the Hong Kong show appeared a couple of days later. Surprise, surprise, it featured a full-page photograph of a scantily-clothed woman wearing boxing gloves. And there were small articles on each of the fights on the show. I was livid when I read the piece on mine: 'Steve Collins is planning a bum-a-month competition' – nothing like what I'd said.

Because of the years I'd spent in America, I wasn't used to dealing with the British tabloid press and this was an important lesson that I was determined not to forget. I got a biro, drew a bra on the woman to make her decent, and stuck the page on my wall to act as a constant reminder not to talk to certain journalists from certain 'newspapers'.

HIGH AND DRY

The most spectacular sight in Hong Kong, for me, was the approach to it in the aeroplane. The air hostess explained to us that it was impossible to make a gradual descent to the airport, because the plane first had to clear the mountains and then get down quickly onto the runway, which, several hundred nervous passengers learned, projects out into the harbour. Unlike most airports, Hong Kong's is not situated in an isolated, rural area. The plane actually makes its descent among the high rooftops of Kowloon, the peninsula on the Asian mainland, and the effect is somewhat similar to landing an aeroplane on Broadway in the middle of New York city.

'High Noon in Hong Kong' was ill-fated from the very moment we arrived in Causeway Bay to discover that nobody had gone to the trouble of organising any training facilities for us. No ring. No punchbags. Not even a skipping-rope. With the fight less than two weeks away, I was shocked at the lack of planning, though I didn't realise, of course, just how much trouble the show's organisers were in.

Beasley, Morrisson, Ruelas and Mercer had started working out at the American Club, but I didn't know quite what I'd do until I found myself explaining my predicament to a complete stranger in the lounge of the Regal Hong Kong hotel one afternoon. 'Oh, I think I might be able to help you there,' he said. 'I know where I could get you a ring, bags, the whole bit.'

There are six million people living in Hong Kong. Of all the people I could have found myself having a conversation with ... Convinced it was wind-up, I asked him where it was. 'On the roof of a skyscraper down-town,' he said.

It was definitely a wind-up.

'No, seriously. There's this French kickboxer I know and he owns it. Uses it all the time to train. I'll show you if you like.' He was telling the truth. On the very top of what must have been a fifty-storey building on the main road to Wan Chai was just what I'd been looking for. It was undoubtedly the most unusual setting I've ever trained in, but it was ideal until the promoters set up a ring for us at the Happy Valley Racecourse, which was a ten-minute walk away from the hotel.

But, it emerged later, Daly and Hemdale Communications had much more worrying matters to attend to than where I sparred and skipped rope every day. Advance ticket sales had been so disappointing that Arum had made a 'buy one get one free' offer, which was unprecedented for a show that contained so many prestigious names. Even the most optimistic predictions said that only 8,000 of the 40,000 seats at the Hong Kong stadium would be filled on the morning of the fight, but there were rumours that only half of those tickets had actually been paid for. There was little interest in the show outside Hong Kong either. Subscriptions to pay-per-view television in the US were poor, probably because there was no big American name on the bill. Tommy Morrison had once been considered the great white hope of his generation, but his credibility had been shattered by his loss to Michael Bentt, who had since been knocked out himself by Herbie Hide. Hide was still unheard of in the States, Beasley was also an unknown quantity and Mercer had as little credibility as Morrisson.

While Daly remained as upbeat as he could, banking on a big walk-up gate on the morning of the fight, it was obvious that he wasn't going to be able to stage the show without sustaining a huge loss. But it was inconceivable that the show would be cancelled. It was still being televised live in the US on HBO Sports. Eight fighters and their entourages had been flown thousands of miles at great expense. The ring was already being erected at the stadium and thousands of extra seats were being brought in. It would probably cost as much money to pull the plug as it would to let it go ahead. And besides, some of the most respected promoters in the sport were there – if the worst came to the worst, it wasn't beyond the capabilities of Bob Arum, Barry Hearn and Micky Duff to put their heads together and rescue it.

FRESH SIGHTS

The English translation of Hong Kong is 'fragrant harbour', but most of the smells you encounter on the streets are far from fragrant. For me, Hong Kong was the ultimate culture shock. Coolie hats. Joss sticks. People crammed into double-decker trams. Noodle vendors. Old Chinese men sitting on crates, offering to tell your fortune, sing you a song or cut your hair for a few dollars. I gazed upwards at the construction workers, running barefoot along narrow bamboo scaffolds twenty or thirty storeys up. One day, I had to put my hand over my eyes to protect them when I saw sparks flying out of a workshop off Pennington Street. I looked in and saw a young lad squatting down as he welded an oil tank onto a motorbike, without goggles or shoes, and holding a conversation with his mates over the sound of the radio. A sacking-on-the-spot offence back in Dublin, I thought, but a way of life out here.

But what I found most extraordinary about Hong Kong was the quite visible extreme between the country's very rich and its very poor. On the waterfront, the country's millionaires lived in mansions that overlooked Victoria Harbour, while just five hundred yards away, hidden discreetly behind the commercial skyscrapers and neon lights, is one of the island's many shack communities, where large families spend their lives crammed into tiny, wooden huts, similar to the ones I'd seen in television reports on the squatter camps in South Africa. Suddenly, the semi back in Romford didn't seem so squalid after all. The saddest thing was that these people didn't even dare to dream about getting something better in their lives. Somewhere along the line, their spirit had been broken and they just came to accept that for Hong Kong to be this great hotbed of capitalism, the country had to have its poorer classes too, they were just part of the equation. The division between the classes was even more stark down in the harbour, where junk boats and sampans, which were home to three or four generations of some families, rubbed shoulders with luxury yachts. Back in the lavish comfort of the Regal Hong Kong hotel, I felt guilty eating dinner after seeing it.

With the Hong Kong skyline providing a spectacular backdrop, the Happy Valley racecourse was the second most extraordinary setting I'd ever trained in (it'll take something very special to beat the French kickboxer's rooftop gym). A ring was erected outdoors and, beside it, a speed ball and heavybag and an area for skipping. The midday heat was stifling, but because my fight was due to start at noon, I did all my training in the morning, when the sun was at its hottest, to try to acclimatise.

But as Freddy and I went to work, something troubled me about the way the show was being promoted, or rather the way I was being promoted. The show had been billed as a Great Britain *versus* United States competition, but no publicity had been given to the fact that there was an Irishman fighting on the bill. The posters for the fight had been printed and pasted on billboards all over Hong Kong before Padilla was forced to withdraw, so none of them bore my name. By the time of the fight, though, I wanted to make sure everyone knew it. I decided to find someone who could sing a quintessential Irish song for me in the ring before my fight. Not 'Amhrán na bhFiann', but the internationally recognised sporting anthem of Ireland, north and south, 'Danny Boy'. There had to be someone among the country's six million inhabitants who knew the words and could hold a tune together. But finding one ...

So when Don Butler, an English journalist who freelances for a couple of newspapers in Hong Kong, phoned me one afternoon for an interview, I asked him: 'Do you want a good story?'

I told him I wanted to host a singing competition in Delaney's, an Irish pub in Wan Chai, and the prize would be the honour of getting into the ring to sing before my fight. 'It would be a huge boost to someone's singing career,' I told him, 'because it will be screened live in America and hundreds of thousands of people will watch it live. Think of that exposure.'

Don was excited about it and word about the competition spread like wildfire. Channel-surfing in the hotel room that evening, I heard my name mentioned on one of the stations: 'Stee-ren Corr-ins is having a singing competition in De-raney's Bar ...'

The next Count John McCormack could be out there tonight, sitting in the living room of his apartment in Shau Kei Wan or Kai Tak, asking the wife: 'Do you think I should give that a go?' Yes, I thought, they're going to be queueing up. And, as it happened, they were. The night of the competition, there was no shortage of entries. There was a shortage of ... well, good ones. From the moment I heard the first contestant straining to get out the opening line I knew we were in trouble. Unfortunately, because I was in training, I couldn't stay until the end and, after taking a small sip from someone's Guinness, discovered how dangerously comfortable I was becoming and knew that if I didn't get back to the hotel soon, I was going to do something I might come to regret by Sunday afternoon. So Des McGahan, an Antrim man who ran an event management company in Hong Kong, said he'd stay on to judge the competition. As I walked down the stairs, the next entrant was taking his turn to slaughter the song – 'From glen to glen, and down the mountainside ...'

Des told me later that the acts got progressively worse, which I found a little bit difficult to fathom. But, he said, he knew a professional singer who'd do it for me.

Frank Bruno arrived in Hong Kong at the same time as I did. Every time I met him, I went away with sore sides. While we'd never actually met before, we didn't need an introduction, because as soon as Frank saw me coming over to him he looked at me, smiled and said: 'Ooohhh, begorra and bejaysus. Top o' the mornin' to ye.'

He'd hail me in the street or in the hotel lobby or in the elevator the same way. 'Well, bless us and save us,' or 'Ohhh, bejaysus.'

One afternoon I remember in particular he was being his normal, obliging self, signing autographs in the foyer when a young Asian man came up and asked whether he could have his photograph taken with him.

'Yeh, sure,' said Bruno.

'Emmm ... Frank, would you mind taking your top off for it?' the guy asked.

Bruno suddenly pushed him away. 'Nah, I don't do none of that kinky stuff.'

While Frank was doing his utmost to keep everyone's spirits high, I was starting to get a bit irritable. While it was necessary to be there to acclimatise, the days were beginning to drag after two weeks in Hong Kong. A couple of hours' training at the racetrack and a couple of hours of running were all I had to break the monotony and the rest of the day was my own. After a fortnight, there were no more adventures to be had. I'd seen everything at least twice already. It was no longer a novelty.

And the star treatment we were receiving back at the Regal Hong Kong hotel was beginning to irk me. For starters, there was the manager, a Frenchman whom Bruno nicknamed 'Merci Beaucoup'. Whenever he saw me, he'd come over, shake my hand (sometimes he'd actually kiss it), tell me what an honour it was to have me in the hotel and then invite me to all kinds of evening soirées. The restaurant was worse. The waiters would pull out my chair for me, fold a napkin and place it on my lap and bow a couple of times. Then they'd disappear into a corner and wait until the water in my glass had dropped within two inches of the bottom and two or three of them would come racing over with jugs to refill it. For the first few days, it was all very gratifying, but now it was beginning to annoy me. Coming towards the end of a meal, I'd put my fork down to take a sip from my glass and the plate would be whipped from under me by the time I looked down, and another one with something else on it put in its place. I just wanted to shout at them: Look, let me have my dinner in peace, will you?

This over-accommodating service was more than just a nuisance. I was trying to watch my weight, which was beginning to cause me concern. It wasn't coming down. Regardless of how hard I worked, I was still finishing training just as I started, eight or nine pounds over the middleweight limit. With a week to go, I was very, very doubtful about whether I'd be able to fight. I couldn't understand why, back in Romford, I could finish training only two or three pounds over, but here, flogging myself in the 95-degree heat, I couldn't even get down to the super-middleweight limit. Someone suggested it might be the richer oils and sauces they use in cooking in Hong Kong, so I started to eat the bare minimum and drink more water. When this fight was over, I decided, I was never going to fight at middleweight again, because I was killing myself. Beasley would make the weight comfortably and would be very strong on the day of the fight. All my overtraining and undereating were going to leave me very weakened.

The tension spilled over at a press conference four days before the fight, where I very nearly made a premature debut in the heavyweight division. The format of the press conference had been explained to me beforehand. Each of us in turn would be called up to the table at the top of the room, sit with our American opponents, give our views to the press, answer a few questions and then get up and leave. Innocuous enough. When my name was called, I walked up with Freddy and we sat down beside Beasley and his manager, Jackie Kallen. In the audience, Ray Mercer, Frank Bruno's opponent, started to make a bit of a nuisance of himself. Every time I tried to answer a question, he was drowning me out with this loud rap: 'Lonny Beasley. New champ, Lonny. Bust his ass, Lonny. You a bad motha. New champ, Lonny. New champ, Lonny Beasley.'

Okay, there's patriotism and there's patriotism, but this was my fight and none of Mercer's business. So when it was over, I went down to where he was standing.

'You've got a big mouth,' I said. Things were getting hot, and Freddy and a few others dragged me away, telling me to leave it be. 'I'd say the same to Mike Tyson if I thought he was out of order,' I said angrily, and I would. There's still a lot in me of that teenage Steve Collins who couldn't turn his back on a confrontation.

Mercer's performance seemed to have fired Beasley with a new sense of confidence. Whenever he walked through the hotel lobby after that, he would break into the Mercer rap himself, screaming wildly: 'New champ, Lonny Beasley,' and 'I'm gonna beat his Irish ass.' Though we'd been staying in the same hotel for two weeks, I hadn't seen Beasley until four days before the fight. But I was already sick of the sight and sound of him. I was going to make him eat his words.

HIGH HEAT

It was hot in Hong Kong. Very hot. And very uncomfortable to work in, though after two weeks I was beginning to grow accustomed to it. The journalists who'd travelled over for the fight developed this fixation about the weather. They'd been told by the local met office that temperatures of between 95 and 100 degrees were forecast for noon on Sunday, the day of the fight. Did the prospect of having to fight in that heat worry me, I was asked.

'No, I'm not going to look for excuses to lose even before I get into the ring. Anyway, I've fought in high temperatures before, when I was in –'

'Yeh, but the ring won't have a protective canopy, you know that?'

'Well, yes, but don't forget Beasley and I will be fighting under the same sun and he'll be just as affected as –'

'Yeh, but what about Barry McGuigan?'

I was waiting for that. McGuigan, of course, wilted in the 125-degree heat of Las Vegas back in 1986 and lost his world featherweight title to

Steve Cruz. I've never believed that the heat was solely responsible for his defeat. Had McGuigan's corner encouraged him to pace himself through the early rounds, instead of telling him to overwhelm Cruz and knock him out, he would never have suffered those two late knockdowns and would have won the fight quite easily on points. As well as this, McGuigan was very dehydrated and was not getting enough fluids into his body. I don't buy this idea that a Mexican, for instance, would find it any easier than I would to fight in the heat of, say, Mexico City. They find the heat just as exhausting and uncomfortable as we do and their bodies can't retain liquids for any longer than we can. Which is why their pace of life is slower, why they work at different times of the day than we do, sit in the shade a lot and sleep for the afternoon. Now, apply that thinking to sport. During the World Cup a few months earlier, there had been a lot of ballyhoo about the Florida heat and how it was responsible for Ireland's 2-1 defeat to Mexico. But Campos, De Olmo and Garcia would have felt the conditions just as badly as Townsend, Staunton and Keane. Except they relaxed, absorbed Ireland's early pressure, scored a goal just before half-time and one just after, and then took a long breather and tried to consolidate what they had.

Unlike McGuigan, I had experience of fighting in these conditions and had been taught how to pace myself and conserve my energy by the Petronellis, who had been through dozens of sparring sessions with Marvin Hagler in the sweltering heat of his training camp in Palm Springs.

While the heat didn't worry me, my ongoing battle with my weight did. Even starving myself and then putting on heavy sweat clothes when I ran, I still wasn't taking off the pounds fast enough and, with just four days to go, I was losing hope.

A few days before the fight, while Bruno and I were training at the racecourse, a white stretch limo pulled up. A VIP had arrived. But who was it? When the car drew up and the driver ran around the side to open the door, out stepped Dame Edna Everidge and her 'bridesmaid', Madge. Des McGahan had arranged the photo opportunity with Everidge and

Bruno to try to drum up publicity for the show. When Bruno showed absolutely no eagerness to break off from his training to go over and meet our famous visitor, Des was in a bit of a sweat. The Dame's ego had been wounded and, for fifteen nervous minutes, dozens of press photographers stood around wondering when he/she was going to snap, turn on her high-heels and go off again. Des turned to me: 'Help me, Steve, will you talk to her?'

'Me?'

'Yeh, come on. You know a boxer's mentality. You could explain to her why he can't allow his training to be interrupted. She'd take it from you.'

So I went over and, after a brief introduction, explained, as diplomatically as I could, that he was in training for a fight and not a pantomime and, while it might appear that Bruno was being ignorant, he was just being professional. Lapsing into Barry Humphries mode, the Dame said he too was a professional and understood perfectly. So we chatted for a while until Bruno climbed out of the ring, towelled off and the two disappeared behind a big huddle of photographers. As Frank's big, booming laugh sounded out above the clicks of the camera flashes, Des came over to me.

'Cheers for that, Steve.'

'What was the problem, Des? She was grand about it.'

'That's what you think. Just before I roped you in, do you know what she said?'

'What?'

'She said: "Does Frank Bruno not know who I am?" '

HIGH FARCE

Whatever good Des was doing in stoking up local interest in the show, the rumours that had re-emerged about Daly's financial problems were undoing it all. Then Barry Hearn arrived. When I heard that he had gone straight from the airport to meet Chris Patten, I wondered whether he was going to try to soften him up for Daly to pop the question about bailing out the show. No, as it turned out, the two were good friends and had probably rubbed shoulders together at numerous Conservative Party functions over the years. Patten had, of course, been the chairman of the party, lost his seat at Westminster in 1992, but had been made Governor of Hong Kong as a reward for helping them defy all the tipsters and win the general election. Hearn was a party supporter. Hardly surprising really, considering that he started to make his way in the world when Margaret Thatcher came to power. He believed in the same values she did – the old-style, self-help policies that had made him a success.

After tea with 'the Guvnor', he breezed into the hotel and, outwardly, looked his usual suntanned and smiling self. Privately, though, he admitted that the show had no more than a 50/50 chance of going ahead. My purse and Herbie Hide's had still not been lodged in his bank account, and he'd given Daly until a minute before the weigh-in, 5.29pm on the Saturday, the day before the fight, to produce it.

It didn't particularly worry me, because there was nothing unusual in any of this. When managers and promoters come together, they like to play politics, sabre-rattle and flex their muscles a bit. But if you see it as anything more than just bluff and bluster, you'll be a nervous wreck by the time you get into the ring. So I wasn't concerned, not even when we discovered that our hotel rooms had still not been paid for and the hotel staff explained to us, in no uncertain terms, that unless we coughed up immediately, our bags were being packed and thrown out onto the streets. I know I said the VIP treatment was beginning to irritate me, but this was a bit too much of the other extreme. 'Merci Beaucoup' must have caught wind of Daly's financial problems, because we hadn't seen him for days now. Anyway, happily, Barry saved me the ignominy of having to live out of a suitcase at the local YMCA for the weekend of the fight, when he charged all of our hotel bills to his own personal credit card.

I was still worried about my weight. When I went to bed the night before the weigh-in, I was still five or six pounds above the limit. Desperate situations call for desperate measures. The day before the fight, I decided to do all the things an experienced fighter knows he shouldn't do to get the pounds off in time for the weigh-in. I put on my sweat clothes and, instead of resting as usual the day before a fight, I put myself through a heavy schedule, didn't eat and then had a sauna. I stepped on the bathroom scales and was bang on the limit. But I felt very, very weak and couldn't wait until the weigh-in was over, so I could get some food and liquids into me.

Hotel foyers are always filled with a great sense of expectation and excitement before a weigh-in. But, coming down the winding staircase, I noticed that the mood in the Regal Hong Kong hotel that day was rather sombre. I met a few of the people who'd travelled from Dublin for the fight. 'Did you hear, it's off?' asked one. No, I reassured him, this was only the promoters playing games. It was brinkmanship. Gemma and I went downstairs to the ballroom, where the weigh-in was due to take place. When I walked in, Hearn, Arum, McGahan and Daly were sitting sullenly at a table at the top of the room. Daly had the microphone: 'My end of the deal was kept. I had to arrange the stadium, air fares and all the pre-flight promotional expenses, which I did, but the purses were not part of my obligation. I've tried desperately to convince my partners to keep the faith. I offered them as much security as I could and it was not quite good enough. It seems I was ready to take the shots, but Mr Arum was not.'

I couldn't believe what I was hearing. The deadline had come and gone and the money still hadn't been lodged in Hearn's account. Just as he'd threatened, he was pulling me and Hide out and, before I'd arrived, Arum had just announced that he was pulling the plug on the entire show.

Tempers started to fray. Accusations were being hurled back and forth and the press conference degenerated into chaos. Estimates of what Daly needed to stage the show varied wildly. Arum said it was $2m. But Frank Bruno's and Billy Schwer's manager, Micky Duff, was livid that his boxers' fights were casualties too, and said that $500,000 would have been enough to save it.

Daly, as it happened, didn't have even that, having already pumped $800,000 of his own money into the promotion. Ticket sales had been so spectacularly bad that the local banks had refused to advance him the $771,000 he said he needed to pay the purses up-front. In desperation, he turned to Arum, whose role in the promotion of the event was suddenly appearing more than a little puzzling. While he was listed in all the fight literature as a co-promoter, he said it was Daly's responsibility to finance the entire event. That wasn't Daly's understanding of the arrangement. He claimed that because all of our contracts were with Arum's company, Top Rank, it was his responsibility to pay us for the fight. Arum held firm and Daly cut a sad, pathetic figure as he made his excuses. 'I wish I could have pulled it off, but I couldn't. I'm very sad for all the boxers who had trained so hard.'

As a last resort, he promised that if we went ahead and fought, we would be paid first thing on Monday morning, as soon as the banks opened and he could get money transferred from Los Angeles.

Incensed at Arum's refusal to bail out the show, Micky Duff was quickly on his feet. He said he had been in the boxing business for forty-five years and he had never cancelled a show just because he was going to lose money. 'I'd sooner cut my throat,' he declared. 'If the show here had made an extra $1m profit, we wouldn't have expected to be paid another penny, but now they find they've made the wrong decision and got the wrong partner and they think they can just walk away from it.'

The reporters were firing questions at Arum, asking why he had been described as a co-promoter on the fight posters, the programme and all the press releases they'd been sent if he wasn't willing to put any financial backing behind it? Listening to all of this, I still expected Hearn and Arum, in some kindly gesture, to say: Okay, listen, tell you what, we'll underwrite the whole thing and make it a success. But the show must go on ... for boxing's sake.

There was to be no knight in shining armour. Hearn was adamant. 'I wouldn't be a proper manager if I let one of my fighters get into the ring not knowing for sure whether they were going to get paid. I do not accept promises. I do not accept guarantees from people I do not know. I do not accept speculation. I have a responsibility to my fighters to ensure that they are going to be paid, and I will be very happy for them to box for Bob Arum when the show is rescheduled.'

Absolutely distraught, I left the room, as the threats of legal action, suits and counter-suits were hurled back and forth. I couldn't believe that everything I'd gone through in the previous six weeks had been for nothing. Every week spent away from my family is a week from our lives destroyed, and I'd spent almost two months in Romford and Norwich, living the life of a monk, every day as ritualised and boring as the one that went before. All the worrying about my weight, the hours I'd spent trying to take the pounds off, it had all been for nothing. I felt like going back in and telling them: We've been bursting our arses for months. You can't just tell us it's off.

But I needed food inside me. I was feeling very weak. Just outside the ballroom, jars of coffee and plates of sweetmeats and cakes had been laid out. Time to replenish the energy I'd lost in training and in the sauna and I ate like a man who hadn't seen food for a month. Then, a voice from inside the ballroom said: 'Billy Schwer to the scales please ...' Oh shit, I thought, as I went to pick up another slice of cake, was the fight back on again? 'Billy Schwer tips the scales at ...'

There was a big rush to the scales, which were behind a 'High Noon in Hong Kong' board at the top of the room, to see what was happening. 'Is it back on?' I asked Hearn. No, he said. They were just going through the formality of weighing-in, so the fighters could say that they fulfilled their side of their contracts when the many legal actions that were being threatened finally came to court. 'So, do I have to weigh-in?' I asked, knowing that I'd have to return to the sauna for a couple of hours after the feed I'd just had. I didn't, he said, because Arum had promised to have my fight rescheduled.

I was angry with Arum. His projected loss from the whole debacle was $750,000, which was a piffling amount to a man whose company was about to promote two of the richest fights in the history of boxing, Michael Moorer *versus* George Foreman and Roy Jones *versus* James Toney. I'm sure that as a former lawyer himself, Arum was legally correct when he said he was not contractually liable to put up our money and bail out the show. In my opinion, he had a moral obligation to do so. All the shouting in the ballroom was being done by the promoters and reporters, but there were eight fighters in there who had trained long and hard for this and who were out of pocket at the end of it.

Not that I blamed Hearn. He was, after all, only protecting my interests. Whenever I hear of a dispute between a promoter and a fighter, my immediate instinct is to side with the fighter, because I've always been a fighter's man. And being a fighter's man, I would never have forgiven him had he allowed me to go ahead with the fight and then come to me on Monday morning and told me that there wasn't any money for me. I was only getting $50,000 for the fight, and it wasn't worth putting everything at risk for that. As I told the reporters when they came looking for my reaction: 'It would have been worse if I'd fought, lost and then found out that I wasn't getting paid.'

I felt for Lonny Beasley, who was explaining to a journalist: 'I'm a meat-and-potatoes fighter. If I don't box, I don't eat. That's the way it is.' He'd taken six weeks off work to train for the fight and was going to have to go back to Detroit to ask his boss for another six. As Jackie Kallen was trying to console him, I decided to have a word. I gave him a hug and said: 'Listen, it'll happen next time, okay?'

As I walked away, I heard him say to Kallen: 'Hey, Collins is a nice guy.'

I didn't want him to think I was a nice guy, because I might start thinking he was a nice guy too. And that wouldn't be good for either of us. Next time we met, he'd be trying to take away everything I'd ever worked for and dreamed of – our house in Castleknock, my family's financial security, the title I'd sacrificed so much for. I'd be trying to destroy his career too. There was no way we could enjoy this kind of relationship before we fought. 'No,' I said, turning around, 'don't make that mistake. This is the other me. The person you see on the night of the fight is the one you're going to have to worry about.'

The people I felt worst for were those who'd travelled from Dublin at enormous expense to see me fight. Stephen Wade, a florist from Dublin, and his father Jack have clocked up of tens of thousands of air-miles, travelling the world to follow my career. I just didn't know what to say to console them. They'd taken the fourteen-hour flight to the Far East and probably spent a couple of grand each just to be there. Yet when I spoke to them, they were just concerned with how upset I was. Others were arriving through the doors of the hotel with their cases hours after the fight had been declared off. Alan and John Keogh, two Cabra lads I used to go to boxing with as a kid, arrived. And I didn't know what to say to Johnny Kenna, the cobbler from Cabra. But he just smiled and said: 'Fuck it, let's get drunk, Steve.' And I couldn't feel sorry for myself when all of these people were taking it so well. At least Gemma and I hadn't paid for our own flights.

I was just as excited about leaving Hong Kong that night as I had been about arriving a fortnight earlier. I was trying to be as philosophical as I could about it. I hadn't earned any money, but I still had my world title belt and a suitcase full of Power Ranger toys for the children, whom I just couldn't wait to see again.

When I got home, I couldn't believe how much Clodagh had changed. It was as though I was looking at a different baby. She had hair now and was much more alert and she seemed to recognise me, which was surprising, considering how little time we'd spent together. It was two months since I'd seen her. If I was counting the cost of Hong Kong in financial terms before, now I realised that the personal cost was far higher. I'd missed eight weeks of her life that I could never get back, just as I'd missed important times in Stevie and Caoimhe's lives. And I'd had six weeks away from Gemma which could never be returned to us. Lost time is something you can't put a price on.

A NEW DATE IS FIXED

Within a couple of days of arriving back in Dublin, I resumed training, determined to keep the momentum going. There must have been something in the 'sauces in the food' theory, because, lo and behold, the pounds started coming off as easily as I'd put them on.

Because it involved a comparatively small amount of money, I knew that my fight with Beasley would be the first on the show to be rescheduled. Within a couple of days, Arum had phoned Hearn to tell him it would be staged at the Boston Garden on 14 December. Now, while a return to my adopted city, this time as a world champion, was an exciting prospect, I knew that my differences with the Petronellis would have to be sorted out before I left or there wouldn't be a fight.

In Dublin, excitement was mounting about Wayne McCullough's fight at the Point Depot against Fabrice Benichou. I've always liked McCullough and, while in Las Vegas during the summer, he'd invited me out to his house for dinner one weekend. So a couple of days before the fight, I went along to the Burlington hotel to wish him well and, over a cup of tea, we had a good laugh reminiscing about our amateur days.

I went to the fight at the Point that weekend, with my friends Brendan O'Carroll and Eamonn Gregg, the former manager of Shelbourne Football Club. I have to say that, in my eight years as a professional, seldom have I experienced an atmosphere like it. It was electric. And the show had been so well organised. While McCullough was receiving his final instructions back in the dressing-room, Brendan was called into the ring to keep the crowd entertained. His first act was to call me in to join him: 'The only Dub to ever win a world title – Steve Collins!'

The noise was deafening. In America, I'd been at shows with three times as many people than were at the Point Depot that night, but the noise didn't compare to this. Quite literally, the hairs on the back of my neck stood on end. I climbed through the ropes and Brendan gave me a hug and then, with me standing beside him, he went through his repertoire of boxing jokes.

The fight itself was incredible. Benichou matched McCullough for aggression and it made for an absolute war.

Afterwards, I kept thinking about the reception I'd received. Barney Eastwood read my mind when he came up and told me: 'Steve, they love you. You have to fight here.'

I heard rumours in Dublin that Hearn had been making inquiries about available dates at the Point Depot in January and February and wondered whether he had some kind of surprise in store for me.

I THINK CHRIS EUBANK HATES ME

Because it had been six months since I'd brought home some proper wages, the work that Sky Television were continuing to give me was very welcome. Not only was it bringing in a few bob, it was also helping to heighten my profile in Britain. And one commentary, in the middle of November, brought me into a very public slanging match with Chris Eubank. I was back in the studio in Hounslow, sitting with Paul Dempsey, offering my opinion of Roy Jones' victory over James Toney the night before. Up until that point, Toney had been mooted as a future opponent for Eubank. During an ad break, Dempsey said that Eubank had agreed to do a live telephone link-up and would be giving his assessment of the fight live when we returned.

'Chris, I have Stephen Collins here with me as well,' Dempsey said.

'Yeth [yes],' said Eubank. There was no 'Hello, Steve,' or 'How are you doing?' It was just 'Yeth'.

I asked Dempsey whether Eubank could hear me and he said he could. 'Hi, Chris, how's it going?' I said.

'Fine.'

'So what happens now? You were supposed to fight Toney and now Jones has beaten him. Will you fight Jones instead?'

'Shall we wait until the interview starts before we start talking about these things?' he said.

'Sorry, I was just asking you off the record.'

When we returned after the break, Dempsey asked him a few very simple questions. I noticed that, in answering them, Eubank would sometimes use five sentences to say things that could be quite adequately covered in one. At the end, he made some reference to the photograph of him on the screen not being good enough and then he turned his attention to me.

'Let me just say ... Let me just say ... Steve Collins?'

'Yeh?'

'Em ... you just keep on doing what you do best in criticising. Sitting there in that seat there, commentating on these fights. But to be a commentator, you must become ... you must be a critic. Em, this is not a good thing. Maybe you should have a good think about what you are doing, sitting there ...'

I was stunned, because it was completely unprompted. 'Well, first of all, I'm not a critic,' I said, 'and I don't criticise you. I've had plenty of opportunity to do it, but I'm not a critic by nature. I'm a fighter and that's what I do best ...'

'What, sitting in that seat, there, sitting in that seat there, you are not criticising?'

Sensing that it was about to get out of hand, Paul Dempsey interrupted. 'I have to cut you short there, Chris.'

'I never criticised you,' I said to Eubank. 'You're wrong – get your facts right.'

By now, Dempsey was struggling to be heard over our exchanges. Then Eubank's line was silenced.

'It could be the basis for discussion about a meaningful title fight in the future, but for the moment, Chris, thanks very much indeed,' Dempsey closed the debate.

I wondered if Eubank had been taunting me for a reason. He's a very shrewd man, always cautious about what he says. I didn't think he'd agree to a live telephone interview and then draw me into that kind of row without an ulterior motive. Up until that moment I had never anticipated fighting him, because I thought it was a match he'd never agree to. But he had confronted me and tried to make me look stupid in front of millions of viewers and now I wanted to fight him. Then things started to add up. The rumours I'd been hearing in Dublin about Hearn and the Point Depot. As soon as I got off camera, I pulled a handful of change out of my pocket and ran to the nearest payphone to ring Barry at home. He'd been watching and was still laughing. 'Aw roight, Steve?'

'Barry, what was all that about? What's going on?'

'That was brilliant, mate,' he said, still trying to calm himself down. 'Absolutely brilliant.'

'Is he setting me up? Am I gonna fight Chris Eubank?'

'Well, Steve, you know that anything can happen in this game.' And with that cryptic message, he said goodbye and hung up.

My imagination was racing. I was putting two and two together, but it wasn't until a week later that I discovered that I was coming up with the wrong answer. It was announced the following week that Eubank was going to fight Belfast's Ray Close for the third time.

Chapter 7

The Boston 'Flu

WE HURT THE ONES WE LOVE THE MOST

When the credits rolled at the end of the lunchtime episode of the TV soap 'Neighbours', Silky Jones had his signal to get up off the couch and get ready for the gym. His day felt somehow incomplete unless he watched the programme before he went out and then got back in front of the telly by the time 'Home and Away' started at tea-time. In the weeks before a fight, a boxer will get to know his sparring partner's every habit, idiosyncracy, like and dislike. Though it was an enormous relief to me that I never developed his compulsion for Australian soap operas, I was delighted when my old friend from Sheffield agreed to help me prepare for my fight with Lonny Beasley which had been rescheduled for 14 December in Boston.

In the ring, he was a brilliant spar, very mobile with a fast hand-speed and a hard punch too. He was excellent at conditioned sparring, or fighting to specific instructions to imitate another boxer's style, in this case Beasley's. What I appreciated just as much was his company. Back in Sheffield, I knew that he was the kind of ally I needed in my camp, a rock of good sense, a man who'd been through all of the same things I had – training away from his family, suffering defeats and disappointments and hauling himself back again. Even aside from boxing, there were so many other things we had in common. Like me, he played his ghetto-blaster far too loudly and he brainwashed me into liking one particular song which involved the lyric: 'Evah since I was young, I've wanted to be a GANGSTAH.'

And he had a sharp sense of humour too, an all too rare quality in the lives of boxers who are preparing for fights and know only sacrifice and temperance. About a week or so before we left for Boston, someone had taught him the expression '*Tiochfaidh ár lá*', an Irish Republican phrase meaning 'Our day will come.' Now, Silky understood neither the meaning nor the political significance of the words, but that didn't stop him adopting it as a catchphrase, which he'd roll off his tongue in place of anything from 'Hello, how's it going?' to 'Hey, who's used all the hot water in the shower?' The day BBC Northern Ireland sent a camera crew to the gym in Romford to interview Eamonn Loughran, we had to explain the sensitivity of the phrase to him. I just had this horrible vision of watching Loughran's interview on television that weekend and seeing Silky in the background, pounding away on the heavybag while chanting in his north of England accent: 'Chuckey awr law.'

To the outsider, the relationship that a boxer has with his sparring partner might seem strange. Some of the more famous and wealthy fighters change their spars more often than their underwear. But for those of us who can afford only one, he'll become like a soul-brother in the weeks before the fight. Now, many people I've spoken to find it difficult to understand how it's possible to spend an afternoon punching somebody in the head and then sit down with that same person, have a good laugh over dinner and watch the television together that evening.

Again, when you're in that ring, dishing out punishment and often taking it in equal measures, you have to remember that it isn't personal. So when you're up against the ropes with a good friend pounding away at your ribs, you tell yourself that this is business – the business you're in, the toughest business of all. You're in the ring to improve your skills, to practise punches on one another and you hold nothing back. If one of the lads in the gym catches me with a punch, I'll nod and tell him it was a good shot, and if he follows it up with a few more and I'm leaning back on the ropes, trying to avoid punches, I'm thinking: Shit, he's got me in big trouble here, and never: The bastard, he didn't have to hit me that hard, I'm not talking to him later on. I almost had my nose broken in training for Beasley. I've had my ribs cracked and I've damaged my knuckles. When my friends in the gym – Eamonn Loughran, Paul Busby, Gary Delaney – are asked to spar with me, they go all out to do me damage. Afterwards, we sit down and have a cup of tea and compliment one another on particular moves.

I had a bit of an angry exchange of words with Barry Hearn a few days before we left for America when I discovered that Freddy King wouldn't be arriving in Boston until the day of the fight. On 10 December, he'd be working the corner for Eamonn Loughran's WBO welterweight title defence against Manning Galloway. Then, three days later, the day before my fight, Gary Delaney would be defending his Commonwealth title and Freddy had to be in his corner too. After that, he'd fly straight to Boston and would arrive a few hours before the weigh-in, which would give me no time at all to work with him over there. I told Barry it wasn't good enough. An identical thing had happened when I fought Reggie Johnson for the world title almost three years earlier. My trainer then, Bernard Checa, didn't arrive in New Jersey until the day before the fight and I'd spent ten days in America with only a sparring partner to give me advice. Regardless of how experienced you are, you still need someone standing over you in the gym, bawling you out of it when you're not giving enough and telling you when you're making basic errors. Checa, like Freddy, had commitments to other fighters, all of whom needed him as much as I did. However, it wasn't the ideal preparation for me and I often wish I'd argued with Eastwood over it. This time, I decided I was going to fight my corner. I was a world champion and, even if the fight was worth only $50,000, my belt and my family's future were on the line and I thought I deserved better treatment. I managed to convince Barry, who said he'd ask Freddy to miss the Delaney fight and fly to the States on the Sunday.

The most formidable opponent I was going to face in Boston wouldn't be Lonny Beasley. It would be the Petronelli brothers, who were quite entitled under US law to seize my $50,000 purse for the fight as a down-payment on what the court had decided I owed them. Their lawyers had made an attempt to have the judgement registered in England, but I believed this was just a bluff. Henri Brandman, my solicitor in London, had completed my defence and it was served a few days after I returned from Hong Kong. Because I was fighting in Boston within a matter of weeks, efforts had to be made to settle the case before I arrived in the States. The Petronellis' lawyers said they were prepared to compromise. Instead of demanding the full $244,231.15 they would accept $125,000, effectively half of what the court had awarded them. But there were terms and conditions. The schedule of payments was this: that I pay $25,000 or half of my purse (whichever was greater) for my first fight after 1 November; and the entire balance after my second fight, providing my purse was over $300,000 and, if it was less than $300,000 and more than $75,000, that I pay them $75,000 and then pay the difference off my third defence.

All of which meant that when I paid my promoter, my trainer, my sparring partners, expenses, the taxman and the Petronellis, I would probably end up earning no money at all from my first three defences. If I lost the third fight, I'd have to retire from boxing with nothing. Also, agreeing to this meant that I had to admit liability, entitling them to claim this money from me in the US, Britain, Ireland, anywhere in the world. What if I lost my first defence? Where was I going to get $100,000 to pay them the balance? They could come and seize anything I owned or anything I earned at home. Would I end up in jail or in debt for the rest of my life if I signed this piece of paper and then got beaten by Beasley?

It wasn't just the money. Stubborn as I am, I was quite prepared to come to an amicable arrangement to pay them a percentage of my future fight purses if that was the price some American judge said I'd have to pay to resume my boxing career in the US. But I couldn't bring myself to admit that I was wrong and they were right. I told Henri to tell their lawyers that I wasn't happy with their proposal.

With the threat to my purse hanging over me, many people probably considered it very foolish of me to travel to Boston regardless. But I genuinely believed that, without lawyers whispering in their ears, I could talk Pat and Goody into accepting some kind of deal. Ironically, Pat was now training my younger brother, Paschal, who was preparing for his professional debut on the undercard of my fight.

A few days before I left for Boston, I phoned Goody who, I believed, was more sympathetic towards me than Pat. Because I still didn't have a place to train in Boston, I asked him whether it would be all right to train in the old place in Brockton during his evening sessions. 'Of course, Steve,' he said. 'You know you're always welcome.'

A SORT OF HOMECOMING

Nothing could have prepared me for the reception at Logan International Airport. On the flight over with Silky, I spent much of the time wondering whether people in Boston would still remember me. When I lived there, I'd received such good exposure from the newspapers and television stations that it was difficult for me to go out shopping without being beseiged by autograph hunters. But that was years earlier and much had happened in the meantime. The local press seemed to side with the Petronellis in the dispute. And anyway, fight fans in Boston who'd followed Hagler in the early 1980s and me in the late 1980s, now had a new middleweight idol. He was Dana Rosenblatt, a twenty-two-year-old southpaw from Malden, Massachusetts, who was unbeaten in twenty-one fights and was well on course for a shot at a world title.

But I hadn't been forgotten. As we collected our luggage and headed towards the Arrivals gate, we were shepherded through customs like VIPs, with our passports and visas not even checked. I was so staggered by what was waiting on the other side that I think I must have walked through the gate with my mouth open. There was green, white and orange bunting everywhere and a 'Welcome Home Stephen Collins' banner hanging from the ceiling. There was an enormous crowd and three television stations had sent news teams to cover my homecoming. Even an Irish dancing exhibition had been laid on in my honour and I was so excited I danced a reel with them. Goody Petronelli was waiting there too and he greeted me with a hug.

At a local amateur show in Boston that night, I was introduced into the ring as a world champion and it was so satisfying to return with a title belt to the city where I began my career. Sleeping was a big problem that night, not because of jetlag, but because I was so excited about the itinerary I'd been given for the week. The item that really caught my eye was a function the following Monday – the Lord Mayor of the city was going to give me the key to Boston. Appropriate though it seemed that the city which saw the start of my pro career should be first to honour me, I couldn't help but feel that it was a pity that Dublin hadn't done it first after I beat Pyatt. I was surprised to hear that Boston's mayor was not Irish, but Italian!

With all of the media attention that my homecoming was receiving, Pat knew he was going to have to talk to me. There was so much excitement about the fight now that he couldn't just seize my purse without losing face with thousands of fans who were buying tickets, and with the American sports network, ESPN, who were televising the show, and with Bob Arum, one of the most powerful figures in the sport. I still hadn't signed a contract for the fight and if Pat followed through with his threat to take my $50,000, I had no intention of going ahead. The newspapers were filled with stories about my hero's welcome, so Pat, through Goody, suggested a meeting on Thursday afternoon, in his office, at 3pm.

It felt just like old times as I pulled open the heavy door and climbed the three flights of steps to the gym on Wednesday for my first sparring session. The place was just as it had been when I left – the two rings directly in front of the door, the bags and the skipping area beside them and, on the far side of the gym, three rooms – the changing room to the right, Pat and Goody's office to the left and, in the middle, with his name printed on the door in gold letters, was the office of Marvin Hagler, where he stored all his fanmail. The walls were still covered with memorabilia from his career, posters of his greatest fights, photographs, programme covers, advertisements for products he'd lent his name to and, most impressively, behind the far ring, a large, life-size portrait of him with his arms in the air, receiving the adulation of the crowd and a speech bubble from his mouth bearing the words: 'Wow! I love these people, this city.'

I knew just how he felt as Silky and I stripped and got ready to spar. My return to the gym in Brockton where I'd begun my career eight and a half years earlier was considered big news. Three television camera crews and sports writers from all the main newspapers were waiting when I arrived and I was looking forward to putting on a bit of a show for their benefit. But with all eyes and camera lenses focused on the ring, things didn't quite go to plan. The first couple of rounds I sparred with Silky were uneventful enough. Then, in the third, he hit me with a straight right and I felt a crunch inside my gumshield. It felt like one of my front teeth had broken in half and I turned my back and started to take the mouthpiece out. Thinking I was feigning injury, Silky followed up with a few combinations, as we'd been taught in the gym. 'No, Silky, stop,' I said.

The cap from one of my front teeth had come off and was lodged in the mouthpiece. By an extraordinary coincidence, Gerry Maher, who'd been my dentist during the five years I lived in Boston, had turned up to watch me! I threw the bit of the tooth to him. 'Here, can you do anything with that?'

Gerry thought it was hilarious. Having turned up to meet an old friend, he'd ended up with a bit of work for himself. He could fit me in the following day, he said, if I wanted to go along to get the cap refitted. Because I was going to be making a lot of public appearances over the following days, it was important to get it fixed immediately, so I asked Pat Petronelli to postpone our meeting from Thursday afternoon until the evening.

When I got up for my run on Thursday morning, I felt what I thought were the beginnings of a bad cold. I had a sniffle and a sore throat, my joints were sore and my body felt weak. A rest would do me good, I thought, so I decided not to train that evening, but to travel up to Brockton anyway for my meeting with Pat. When I got back from the run that morning, the first thing on my mind was to get into the hotel shop to buy the newspapers and find out what had been written about my return to the old gym. To my horror, and much to Silky's amusement, he'd managed not to only to knock my tooth out of my head but also to knock my name out of the headlines. The press had nicknamed him 'The Tooth Fairy' and he couldn't wait to get back to England to show his friends. I sat on the end of my bed and turned on the television to see what the ABC news had made of it. And their report came on: 'If boxer Steve Collins was looking to impress people on his arrival back in Boston last night, he picked the wrong man to try to look good against ...'

The report ended with a shot of me with this great big, gap-toothed grin. We roared with laughter for about five minutes. With a punch that was hardly strong enough to knock over a storefront dummy, Silky managed to completely upstage me and become a media celebrity in Boston overnight. Not since Henry Cooper put Cassius Clay on the seat of his pants in 1963 had an English boxer been catapulted to such stardom by a single punch!

MAKING IT IN THE STATES

Frank Sinatra was wrong. When he sang that if you make it in New York, you can make it anywhere, it was obvious that he'd never worked as a painter and decorator or builder's labourer back in Dublin. Talking to some of the ex-pats in Boston, I was reminded just how much easier I'd found life in America in the years after I left Ireland. Growing up in Dublin is the perfect grounding for life in the big, bad world. It's the ultimate school of hard knocks. Money is so tight that people, in service industries especially, spend their lives undercutting one another, conning each other and fobbing people off. When they emigrate to cities like Boston, they thrive because they're so streetwise and cunning. A bunch of lads move over there and get a job, for instance, to paint a town hall in a Boston suburb. They overprice the job and then find that they're actually paid half the money before they even open a tin of paint. In Dublin, they'd complete the job and spend six or seven weeks chasing people up to try to get their money.

One ex-pat who helped put bread on my table when I first went to Boston was Marty Ward. Many people will know him as the man who carried the tricolour into the ring for most of my fights in the States. Marty, a publican from the North Circular Road in Dublin, emigrated to Boston a few years before I did, scraped together enough money to buy a ramshackle house, renovated it and sold it, bought a couple more houses with the profits and built up a thriving business. Go to the the Tara Bar in Dorchester any Friday night and at least half of the people drinking at the bar will be on Marty's payroll.

Just as thousands of other Irish had found it easy to get rich in Boston, I found it easy to get famous when I went there. That excited me. I enjoyed seeing myself on television, reading my name in the newspapers and being noticed every time I went out. Even in 1987, a year after I'd turned pro, I was enjoying the kind of fame in Boston that was reserved for Tour de France and Eurovision Song Contest winners back in Dublin. In America, when you achieve something, the attitude is: Hey, well done, Buddy. In Dublin, it's: Well done, you jammy bastard, how can I get what you have? The Americans appreciate winners more. That probably explains why I was getting the freedom of Boston before the freedom of Dublin.

When I beat Kevin Watts to win the US Boxing Association title, the significance of it wasn't really appreciated back in Dublin. My brother Roddy told me about the night I phoned him to tell him. It was the early hours of the morning back in Ireland, but I was too excited to wait until he was up. 'I'm going to be a world champion, Roddy,' I told him, with the belt laid out across my lap.

'There's no need to tell me that, Steve. I know you will be.'

'I'm gonna do it.'

'Fair play to you, Steve.'

The conversation over, Roddy put his head back on the pillow. 'Who was that?' said his wife, Caroline.

'It was Steve. Said he's going to be a world champion.'

Roddy found it a little difficult to believe at the time. He's honest about it now, but it wasn't until he went over to watch my first defence against Tony Thornton and returned to Dublin to start spreading the word, that I began to get the credit I deserved back home. In America, though, it was coming easy to me. Fame appealed to me, because I wanted, and still do want, to be a legend. I grew up idolising Marvin Hagler and I want young children who are boxing to look up to me in the same way.

CONFRONTATION

I couldn't wait to get my meeting with Pat over and done with. I'd been in the gym for about half an hour before he arrived and we went into his office to talk. I got an idea of his mood when he told me to sit down and took up a position on the other side of his desk. He put his left hand in his jacket pocket, fiddled about for a bit, took it out and then started talking. If he had a dictaphone in his pocket, I was very amused at his amateurish attempt to conceal it.

'Have you got a tape recorder in your pocket, Pat?' I asked.

'Of course I have,' he said. Then he laughed and denied it. From his right pocket, he pulled out what he thought was his trump card, a folded up piece of paper which I didn't bother reading when he threw it down on the desk. He told me that if he wished he could call the cops to arrest me. The irony of this was not lost on me. I was being threatened with imprisonment in the same week as I'd been offered the freedom of the city! On Monday, the Lord Mayor might have to bring the key to Boston to the state penitentiary.

Of course, it was an idle threat. I said to him: 'Pat, the way I look at it, there are two scenarios. You can either get me thrown in jail or you can threaten to take my entire purse for the fight. Either way, I don't give a fuck.'

I didn't care because he had to be bluffing. If he threatened to take my money, I was walking out and he'd have a lot of difficult questions to face from some of the most influential figures in the sport. As well as that, to the Boston public, he'd be the wealthy boxing trainer who was persecuting a popular fighter trying to earn a half-decent living for his family. But he still seemed a little surprised that I hadn't broken down in tears at the threat of spending time in prison. So he tried to reason. Our dispute, he said, had cost him an enormous amount in legal bills and his solicitors needed to be paid.

'Well, I'll pay them,' I suggested, 'and we'll make up and do business together. Pat, I've only got a few more years left in boxing, but when I finish, I'm going to go into training and managing myself and we can work together. I'll put your fighters on my shows. It's not doing any of us any good allowing this row to continue. Let's just call a press conference and say it's over.'

Pat then tried emotion. I'd broken his heart four years earlier, he told me, walking out on him when he had big plans for me.

'Pat,' I told him, 'these last four years, they've been wasted years. But it's all lost time. There's nothing we can do to get that back. What we can do is work together to ensure we don't lose any more.'

He seemed to be not so much so concerned with the money the court had awarded him but with the millions of dollars he might have got had I stayed on. No, he wanted his pound of flesh.

'You don't need the money, Pat. I mean, $100,000 to you is like $1m to me. I've had seven fights in the last two years and I've got shit out of them. After this fight, I won't be fighting for less than $200,000. When I'm in the big money, Pat, then we can work out an arrangement.'

'You have a house, don't you?'

'What?'

'You own a house back in Dublin?'

I didn't. But I couldn't believe that Pat, having watched me sweat buckets in the gym for years, trying to become a world champion and to build a future for myself and my family, was suggesting that I sell our family home to pay him.

'I don't even own a house. We're renting one in Castleknock ...'

His attention returned to my purse for the fight. 'I can't believe you're fighting for $50,000. Why are you fighting for so little money?'

'If they'd offered me a quarter of a million dollars for this fight, I wouldn't have taken it.'

'Why, what are you talking about?'

'Because if I'd been earning that for it, you'd have taken it. You'd have instructed your lawyers to have that money seized. Now, because it's only $50,000, you wouldn't bother. Because you know I'd never come back here to fight again and you wouldn't get a cent more.'

The conversation was becoming repetitive, so I suggested one last time that I might pay off his legal bills and call it quits. 'There are too many people in our ears, Pat, telling us what to do. I could have a million pounds in the bank now and still not be able to buy back those years we lost. But we can work together in the future for both of our benefits.'

Forty-five minutes after we disappeared into the office, we re-emerged no closer to settling our differences than before. He said he'd talk to his lawyers and call me at the hotel the following day. I knew that they'd tell him not to buckle and to take me for every cent he could get.

DOWNHILL FAST

My condition was deteriorating rapidly. The following morning, my head felt light, my arms and legs heavy and I couldn't summon up the energy to run. I was very concerned. In all of my career, I've never felt in better shape than I had leaving for Boston. Maybe I'd overtrained. My preparations for this fight had been longer than ever before, having spent six weeks in the gym preparing for Hong Kong and then another seven for Boston. I wondered what effect my struggle to get down to the weight limit in Hong Kong had had on my body. I wasn't eating properly, was far below my natural body weight and was therefore more susceptible to colds and 'flus. And the winter in Boston was a particularly cold one. I needed more rest, so I cancelled training that day too.

I decided to get some penicillin to see if that would help. Looking back, it was foolish of me not to go to see a doctor at this stage, but I figured that, once I got the drugs inside me, I'd be all right by the time Freddy King arrived from London on Sunday evening.

The promoter of the fight, Al Valenti, had arranged a car for me to drive downstate to training every night. But before I could collect it, I had to get my American driving licence renewed. The shamrocks that I'd had reshaved into my hair attracted some attention in the Department of Transport office and people recognised me as 'that boxer guy who got his tooth knocked out'.

Then one of the state troopers came out and asked me to step into his office. I thought I must be in trouble. I hadn't left America with a parking fine outstanding or something, had I? He pulled out a large, leather-bound book. 'Can I ask you for your autograph?'

I signed my name and stapled my old driving licence to the page opposite. Silky and I couldn't believe how many people recognised us, at toll booths, supermarket queues, traffic jams, restaurants, even the launderette.

Back in my hotel room, the little red light on the phone was flashing to tell me that a message had been left for me. Pat Petronelli had phoned, so I called him back. The conversation this time was blunt. 'Steve,' he said, 'I'm not sending you to jail, don't worry.'

'Oh thanks, Pat,' I said sarcastically.

'I'll call you again.'

He didn't mention whether he was going to take my money for the fight. At that stage it didn't matter much anyway. My 'flu was getting worse and my chances of being well enough by the following Wednesday evening were diminishing. The promoters had given me a pretty hectic schedule of appearances that I was supposed to work around my training schedule, but as I retired to my sick bed, I knew that they'd all have to be cancelled. The following day, a Saturday, I was supposed to attend a horse race at the Suffolk Downs race track, where the 3.25 had been named after me. I was sorry to miss it. I spent the day in bed intead, still confident that a few days' rest would cure me.

The unpleasantness with Pat and my illness had distracted me from the real reason why I was in Boston. Lonny Beasley was conspicuous by his absence again, just as he had been in Hong Kong. This time, though, he did almost all of his training at home in Detroit and flew up to Boston the weekend before the fight. I'll never forget the first time I saw him in the hotel. Having played pool in the bar downstairs to kill a few hours in the afternoon, Silky and I were walking back up to the reception area when he suddenly came through the revolving doors. Silky continued chatting away, his back to Beasley, but whatever he was saying, I didn't hear any of it. I was glaring over his shoulder at this man who wanted to take away everything I'd ever worked for. I hated Lonny Beasley at that moment.

A worried look came over Silky's face. 'Oh, fuck, Steve? Steve, what's the matter? Did I say something wrong?'

I nodded towards the other end of the reception area and Silky spun around. 'Oh, it's Beasley. Fucking hell, Steve, you frightened the life out of me then. I thought you were giving that look to me.'

'It didn't look like you at all,' he told me later. 'You were like a stranger. This hatred came over your face. I don't know what you did to Beasley, but you scared the shit out of me.'

My main reason for going to the gym that night was to ask a favour of Goody. I wanted him to work in my corner alongside Freddy on the night of the fight. Because they were the biggest influences on my professional career, it would mean a lot to me to have both of them in my corner when I went into the ring as a world champion for the first time. Goody seemed honoured, but asked how Freddy would feel about it. I said I didn't foresee any problems. While he didn't expect to be in the corner proffering advice between rounds, Goody was a proud man and didn't want to be there just to hold the slops bucket either. I suggested that, when Freddy arrived the next day, the three of us should sit down and discuss a role for him.

I didn't spar that night either. After changing, I skipped, shadow boxed and then pawed at the heavy-bag for a while. However, I was feeling listless and gave up. I decided to spend Sunday morning and afternoon in bed, in the hope that I'd be better again by the time Freddy flew in that evening.

RAGING BULL

Being back in Boston reminded me of the night in 1990 when I'd had my last fight at the Garden and almost came to blows with one of the legends of the ring. Jake La Motta was guest of honour and ring announcer for my fight against Eddie Hall. He was approaching seventy at the time, but was still every bit as menacing and intimidating as Robert de Niro's film portrayal in *Raging Bull*, which I had always presumed was exaggerated until I met the man himself. When I was introduced to him at the pre-fight function, he just stared at me, with a spiteful look in his eye. 'I wish you'd been around in my day,' he said.

'Why?' I asked.

'Because you gotta pretty face and my wife would have loved ya. And I'd have loved beating you up.'

Then he grabbed Gemma in a playful hug. 'And I'd have taken her from you as well.'

But he seemed a bit serious. 'Hey, you're an old man, calm yourself down,' I said.

It was the following night, though, that I thought he was going to invite me outside for a brawl in the carpark. I never found the spark in my fight with Hall, but still got a comfortable decision after ten rounds. At the press conference, La Motta was asked by a reporter what he thought of me. 'He didn't impress me,' was his abrupt reply.

The press seemed delighted. 'Did you hear that, Steve?' another reporter asked, 'you didn't impress Jake La Motta. What do you say to that?'

'Well,' I said, 'Jake La Motta has been married to some of the most beautiful women in the world and they didn't impress him either. What chance have I got?'

There was a loud roar of approval, peals of laughter and then a round of applause. From the look on his face, La Motta didn't take too kindly to being upstaged and I really thought he was going to ask me to step outside. I thought about him later on that night and was just grateful I wasn't around in the late 1940s and early 1950s, when he was a world champion, because we'd have taken lumps off each other and not necessarily in the ring either.

We met him again at breakfast the following morning. He was already sitting at a table on his own and Gemma and I joined him. With no reporters and photographers to play up to, he was as meek as a lamb. As we ate our cereal and drank coffee, I actually got to enjoy his company. He told me about the infamous three- and four-day drinking binges he used to go on with another boxing legend, Rocky Graziano. Though they were both middleweight boxers from the same era, they would never fight one another because they had both come from Italian ghettoes in New York and were good mates. La Motta remembered that, after one particularly heavy session, he woke up next to Graziano in an alleyway somewhere in The Bronx. 'Hey, Rocky,' he said, staring up at the sky. 'Is that the sun or the moon I see up there?'

'I don't know, Jake,' replied Graziano, 'I'm not from around here.'

And he told me all about Robert De Niro, whom he'd worked with in the making of the movie. Now, De Niro is one of my all-time favourite actors and what La Motta told me just reinforced my view of him. He was an excellent mimic as well as a great actor, he told me. He picked everything up, even the tiniest little quirks in La Motta's personality, so quickly.

The film had allowed La Motta to be reborn and not just in celluloid either. Until it was made, he was out of work and had frittered away all the money he'd earned during his career. Now, he explained, he was still broke, but he didn't need money. 'Where do you come from? Dublin?' he asked. 'If I wanted to go to Dublin tomorrow, someone would make a call for me and I'd be flown over and put up in a top-class hotel and I wouldn't have to spend a penny. I don't carry money with me. I don't have none. But I don't need none neither.'

After meeting him, I knew better than ever before that I was going to have to start earning some serious money, in case a very wealthy film director didn't make a movie about me and bail me out late in life.

SICK LEAVE

It's easy to be wise after the event. The penicillin and the afternoon in bed did me no good at all. I actually felt worse as I drove to the airport to meet Freddy King and my mother, who were on the same flight from London. The flight was delayed, so I went to the coffee shop in the arrivals lounge, where I met my brother Paschal, his girlfriend Joan, and Marty Ward (who had now included Paschal on his payroll, along with about 95 percent of Boston's other first, second and third-generation Irish!).

It was in the airport that I first realised I was going to be in no condition to fight. During the hour and a half we spent waiting for the flight, I was coming down with hot flushes, and had to go outside to get some air. When Freddy and his son, Jason, saw me, they knew too. But I put a brave face on it and told them I'd make my mind up about it after a few rounds of sparring that night. Tired though he was after all his travelling, Freddy wanted to drive straight to the gym to see just how bad I was. We piled his luggage into the back of the Cherokee and headed south on the motorway towards Brockton. The conversation on the way there was about Eamonn Loughran, who had blown away Manning Galloway the previous night. Apparently, in his interview afterwards, he'd mentioned Silky's name several times. He said he had looked so sharp only because of his excellent sparring partner who had given him so many tough rounds in training, and ended it by saying: 'Silky Jones was a much tougher opponent and a much better fighter than Manning Galloway.'

Silky was delighted. An obscure club fighter one week, now he had a reputation on both sides of the Atlantic. He deserved it.

During the drive to the gym, I asked Freddy whether he'd be prepared to work with Goody on the night of the fight. A bit uncertain at first, I think he felt I was shoving him out until I assured him that he would still be my number one. Goody would be there, not to give me instructions or tend to cuts, but ... well ... just to be there.

When we arrived, Freddy and Goody got acquainted, while Silky and I got changed and climbed into the ring for a six-round sparring session. After four rounds, I was hardly strong enough to hold my arms up and Freddy was standing at the side of the ring, shaking his head. The session was abandoned and we all went into Goody's office to talk. 'There's no way you're fightin' on Wednesday, Steve,' Freddy said.

This was a bit hasty, I said. There were three more days to go before the fight. I could wake up the next morning and feel fine. But I was deluding myself. Even if I made miraculous progress that night, I hadn't trained for days. I kept thinking about the thousands of people who'd bought tickets and all the excitement that my 'homecoming' had generated. And the plans to give me the key to the city. I'd been in training since August for this fight, almost four months away from my family and now I was going to have to come to terms with the fact that it was off for the second time.

The atmosphere was strained, to say the least, as we drove back to the hotel. Too upset for conversation, I just kept telling Freddy I understood. But he knew that, given half the chance, I'd fight just to keep everyone else happy. Then a bit of a row broke out when I told him about the penicillin. In the past, he had given us numerous lectures about what to do when we felt the first symptoms of a 'flu. 'Get a boostah injection,' he'd say. When I told him I hadn't bothered, he flipped. 'I've told you time and time again abaht that, Steve. No wondah you're not gettin no bettah.'

'Look, Freddy,' I said, 'I've been over here on my own for the last few days with all this shit with Pat Petronelli hanging over me and I've had to train on my fucking own. Now, I know it's not your fault and you'd have been here if you could, but I think I've done all right by myself. Okay?'

For ten minutes nobody said another word, until I finally broke the silence by apologising to him and he said sorry to me. We decided not to tell the promoter, Al Valenti, until we had a proper medical opinion of my condition and the following day, we drove back to Brockton to see a local practitioner, Doctor Behige Asaker. After examining me, he decided I was suffering from a virus – and a particularly debilitating one at that – and prescribed some antibiotics. I spent the rest of the day in bed, with the phone off the hook, too tired and depressed to explain to people what was happening.

Besides, I wasn't quite certain myself. When I told Valenti I was going to have to withdraw, he insisted that I went to see Dr Joel Solomon, the medical commissioner. Before any official announcement was made that my fight was off, he wanted a second opinion to verify my story. This annoyed me at first, because I was being made to feel like a liar. I hadn't spent four months in training and travelled half way across the world for a meagre $50,000 fight only to feign an illness a couple of days before. But, when I thought about it, if the main bout on the show was going to be called off, hundreds of people were going to want their money back and Valenti did need certification for insurance purposes. I was told to keep the story under wraps until I saw Dr Solomon on Tuesday, the day before the fight. This meant locking myself in my room and not letting anyone see me, because with my face looking pale and drawn, it would be obvious to anyone that I was in no fit state to fight.

THE BEST-LAID PLANS ...

It broke my heart to have to cancel my appointment at the Lord Mayor's office. As it turned out, though, he'd had to leave town unexpectedly on business that day, and his office had phoned to ask whether I'd be happy if his deputy presented me with the key. So I used that as an excuse not to go and said that I'd collect it from the mayor himself the next time I was in Boston. They didn't suspect a thing.

But the Irish journalists were becoming increasingly sceptical. They'd been in Boston for more than twenty-four hours and, with the fight only two days away, had still not seen me. That night, I'd failed to show up at the Boston Celtics' basketball match, where I was supposed to come out on the court at half-time to be introduced to the crowd, along with Dana Rosenblatt, who was fighting on the undercard. I also cancelled my plans to appear as a guest on a game show on the Sports Channel. I didn't have any choice really. I couldn't go on live television and start talking about the fight, knowing very well that there wasn't going to be one.

Tired of fobbing off questions, Freddy came into my room in the early hours of Tuesday morning and said that the journalists from the Irish papers were downstairs and I was going to have to talk to them. I called them up to the room and told them there was a very serious doubt over the fight because I was ill. No final announcement would be made, though, until I'd seen the medical commissionser.

Freddy reckoned I was suffering from one of those viruses that athletes contract when they overtrain. It was plausible enough. Dr Solomon nailed that theory the following day. 'You have a streptococcal infection,' he said after taking a blood test at his surgery in Winchester. 'You're a very sick man. There's no way you should fight.'

When we got back to the hotel, we phoned the Virgin Air desk at Logan International Airport and made arrangements to fly out of Boston that evening. Before I went, though, I decided that I owed it to the seven thousand people who'd bought tickets, and to Lonny Beasley, who'd spent another six pointless weeks in training, to offer an explanation personally. I also apologised for making myself incommunicado for the previous few days. At the end, I wished Dana Rosenblatt luck in his fight with Frank Savannah, which was now top of the bill, and expressed the hope that, one day soon, I'd return to Boston to fight him.

I was upset that I wasn't going to be there when Paschal made his professional debut that night, but he understood that it wouldn't be good protocol for a man who'd been struck down by a virulent infection to be seen at ringside.

It had been another wasted journey. Not only for me either. Johnny Kenna, the cobbler from Cabra who had turned up in Hong Kong, had now flown to Boston as well. It took us some time to convince him that the fight really was off again. I felt for him, and also for Freddy and

Jason, who had hardly slept in forty-eight hours and didn't have time to overcome the jetlag when they were flying back across the five time zones again. A few hours before they left, though, they made a 'pilgrimage' to Boston's top tourist attraction – the Bull And Finch Bar, which is the inspiration behind the sit-com 'Cheers'. An absolutely fanatical fan, Jason led Freddy, Silky and Johnny across the city on the underground to the bar on Beacon Street, while I stayed behind in the hotel room, packing my bags. They enjoyed lunch there and the few pints that followed. Jason came back with a bag full of souvenirs and seemed to enjoy the afternoon, even if his father did embarrass him by raising his glass to each and every person who walked past and saying: 'Cheers.'

Our bags were stacked by the door and I was returning the last of the calls that had built up while I had made myself unavailable. I'd just put the receiver down on a journalist with RTE radio when there was a loud rap on the door. Freddy answered it and was confronted by a man in a dark navy suit. Now, possibly the most costly lesson I've learned during my boxing career is that when you see a man in a dark navy suit approaching, it's advisable to hide, because he's more than likely trying to serve you a writ. It was too late. He'd already seen me. 'Steve Collins?' he said.

'Yeh?' I answered, fearing the worst.

'I'm the manager of the hotel,' he said, and pulled a sweatshirt from behind his back, 'and we'd like you to have this, courtesy of the hotel. Thanks for staying, you were a great guest and please come again.'

GOOD NEWS, BAD NEWS

And I had every intention of going back again, optimistic as I was that the fight would be rescheduled for early in the New Year. It wasn't until I got back to Dublin that I learned that I'd probably never be able to fight in the States again. It was late on Wednesday night when the phone in the kitchen rang. It was George Kimball, a good friend and journalist with the *Boston Herald*. He told me that Pat Petronelli had a big surprise planned for me on the day of the fight. He was planning to seize my entire

$50,000 purse. Not only that. He was also demanding the purses of the other fighters on the bill too, which, apparently, he was legally entitled to do. Unknown to me, his lawyers had gone to court earlier in the week to file the documents and were preparing to serve the papers on the day of the fight. The court orders could be served on co-promoter Bob Arum as he stepped off the plane at Logan airport on the day of the fight, to Barry Hearn at ringside that night and to Al Valenti, the other co-promoter, at the Canal Street ticket agency owned by his father.

Now, there was never any question of me fighting for nothing. I had not signed the contract for the fight. I'd have simply got dressed, walked out of the dressing-room and caught the next plane out of the country. Now I had to accept that, while I'd told so many of the journalists in Boston that this was the city in which I wanted to end my professional career, because of Pat Petronelli I'd almost certainly never be back there to fight again.

There was a great deal of scepticism in Boston about my illness. A few of the newspapers suggested that I had feigned it just for an excuse to pull out of the fight because of Petronelli's threat to take my money. Though this was patently untrue – and I've got medical certificates to prove it – I didn't complain, because these stories suited me. Pat was being cast as the villain and all the coverage might bring about pressure for a re-examination of the case. The *Boston Sunday Herald* called for just that ten days later.

The only good news was that Paschal won his fight. I was disgusted to find out that he was very lucky to have fought at all. Having spent five hours in the dressing-room, being told at regular intervals: 'You're on first', 'You're on second', 'Get ready, you're on next' and 'Sorry, Paschal, you're not on until the end of the show', he was eventually told that they couldn't fit him in and that he'd have to make his professional debut some other night. A pro debut is something special. Realising how important it was, my mother had flown to Boston just to be there with him. Like me, Paschal had been restless for weeks before his first fight, had thought of nothing else. He was eating the right foods, going to bed early, getting up early, slogging his guts out in the gym and making all the necessary sacrifices. Now, when he was changed, gloved up and ready to box, they were telling him to go home and come back some other time. This was typical of how undercard fighters are treated.

It was only after some remonstration from Marty Ward and Gerry Callan, a journalist with the *Star* in Dublin, that Al Valenti relented and agreed to put his bout on at the end. After spending five hours sitting on the rubdown bed in the dressing-room, Paschal wasted no time in the ring and knocked out his opponent, Francisco DeJesus, in twenty-four seconds. That was the official time, anyway. There were some suggestions that it may actually have happened in eight seconds. It was certainly caused by the first and only punch of the fight and Paschal, in causing the quickest-ever knockout in the history of the Boston Garden in the very last fight ever to be staged there (the old Garden was about to be demolished) went on to a local pub to celebrate making boxing history twice in one night.

Soon after I got home, I got a call from an old friend in America, Jim Sullivan, who's involved in film production in Hollywood. He had a proposition to put to me and I listened eagerly. An all-Irish show was being planned for Boston, featuring me, Wayne McCullough, Michael Carruth and a few other Irish fighters, possibly Eamonn Loughran or Ray Close. It would be dubbed The Donnybrook, which as well as being a village in Dublin is also an Irish-American slang word for a free-for-all. While I hardly needed to be reminded about the Petronelli stumbling block, I was intrigued and asked who was behind it.

'A guy called John Daly. He's in charge of a company called Hemdale.'

Whether he was aware of my previous involvement with Hemdale, I wasn't sure. So I told him that he'd have to talk to my manager, Barry Hearn. I told Hearn about it and he said that, if the money was lodged in his bank account beforehand, he'd be more than happy for me to fight on Daly's show. But in the weeks that followed, other events would overtake it.

CHAPTER 8

A Strange Kind of Calling

'HELLO, FRANK, IT'S STEVE COLLINS ...'

The disappointment of having travelled several thousand miles to two continents and back without fighting and without earning a single penny left little cause for festive cheer in our house. But I was determined that it wasn't going to spoil Christmas for us. On Christmas Day, I kept the promise I'd made years earlier to the children, when we drove down to the stables on our plot of land to discover that Santa Claus had left two ponies there.

For some reason, winters are bad times for me. In December, January and February I'm always at a low ebb, either frustrated, depressed or ill. As 1993 drew to a close, I was all three. Hardly an hour went by when I didn't think about those seven wasted months. Beating Chris Pyatt was supposed to change my life. Being a world champion lifted an enormous burden from me and made me feel somewhat more fulfilled. But in the workaday currency of pounds, shillings and pence, I was no better off than I'd been twelve months earlier. At thirty, I didn't need to be reminded that I didn't have too many miles left on the clock.

Spending days in bed, struggling to get over an infection, gives you time to think. It helps you to see things more clearly – the wider picture, the greater scheme. Whiling away the days before Christmas, lying under a mountain of blankets, I thought about the direction my career was heading. I was third in the pecking order at Matchroom, after Chris

Eubank and Herbie Hide. As long as I stayed in that position, I was never going to earn the kind of money that would allow me to retire in comfort by the age of thirty-five, with all my faculties still intact. The only way I was going to any real money was by beating Eubank, who was never going to agree to fight me. And even if he was, he had a £10m deal to fight for Sky Sports. While he was raking in the money for Matchroom, why would Barry Hearn risk the life of the goose that lays his company's golden eggs by sending him out to do twelve rounds with me?

Two days before Christmas, I decided that my career needed a shot in the arm and I started to think about looking for a new manager. To the outsider, this attitude might seem a little mercenary. But it isn't at all. In football, contracts can be bought and sold and players move on and get better deals for themselves. Like footballers, boxers are nothing more than commodities, figures in a ledger. While Hearn and I were on good terms, my greatest loyalty had to be to my family and to making the future a little easier for them than the past nine years had been. It took me all of those years to learn a very fundamental rule in the boxing business: you should like your manager, but love your wife. That's the greatest advice I can give to people who choose this profession.

Of all the managers I could have approached, I chose Frank Warren, whose handling of the arrangements for my fight against Pyatt had caused me such misery. At the time, I thought he was the biggest bastard alive – but seven months later, reflecting on it rather more coolly, I understood that he had no personal ill-feeling towards me. In fact, he had no personal feelings towards me whatsoever, which was why I decided to phone him first. When I got through we talked like two old friends at a school reunion. Then, opting for the direct approach, I explained my situation to him. How I hadn't earned a penny since the day I beat Pyatt. How Sky Sports would pay me to commentate, but not to fight. How I wasn't going to make any *real* money unless I could get fights against people like Eubank and Nigel Benn. What I needed was a clean break to wipe out all the frustrations of the previous seven months.

'Frank,' I said, 'I know a lot of stuff went on between us in the past,

ABOVE: My arrival in Hong Kong to defend my WBO middleweight title against Lonny Beasley proved something of a culture shock. Here I take in the sights in Wan Chai. BELOW: Training at the Happy Valley racetrack.

ABOVE: My weight caused me problems in Hong Kong, but I still had time for some light entertainment with Dame Edna Everidge and her 'bridesmaid', Madge. BELOW: Another celebrity photo-call. This time Gemma and I enjoy a moment with Frank Bruno in the Regal Hong Kong hotel.

The show can't go on: journalists listen to my reaction to the news that the 'High Noon in Hong Kong' show has been cancelled just a minute before the weigh-in.

Sartorially elegant, I arrive in traditional Irish dress for the press conference to announce details of my fight with Chris Eubank.

ABOVE: I respond to Eubank's comments about Africa by questioning his commitment to his roots, while Barney Eastwood (left) and Barry Hearn (centre) wonder what will happen next. BELOW: Eubank storms out, promising a 'fight to the death', as Eastwood tries to calm him down.

ABOVE: **All work no play – I stop to catch my breath and to rewind my Tony Quinn cassette outside O'Shea's Casino during the weeks I spent preparing in Las Vegas.** (PHOTO: LAWRENCE LUSTIG / DAILY STAR) BELOW: **The warrior prepares for battle my – headguard is fastened for another sparring session in the gym.**

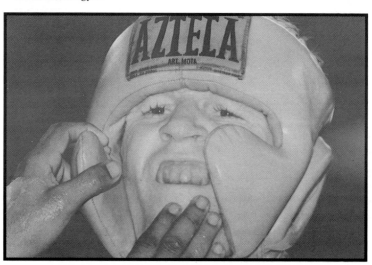

Gemma, Clodagh, Caoimhe and Stevie keeping a check on how my training is progessing in Vegas.

For every punch Eubank threw, he found two in his face and he knew that I wasn't just another opponent.

ABOVE: **After withstanding relentless pressure, Eubank finally crumbled in the eighth round when he was hit by a body shot.** BELOW: **Looking indignant, he contemplates being put on the seat of his pants for the first time in three and a half years.**

Eubank still found the strength to knock me down with a beautiful punch in the tenth round, but a smile to my trainer Freddie King in my corner indicated that I was all right. (PHOTO: LAWRENCE LUSTIG / DAILY STAR)

ABOVE: I survived the knockdown to put Eubank under pressure in the eleventh round, (PHOTO: BILLY STICKLAND/ INPHO) **and (BELOW) rocked him with just over a minute to go.** (PHOTO: LAWRENCE LUSTIG / DAILY STAR)

A night when greatness told: I hold aloft the WBO super-middleweight title belt, after becoming the first man ever to beat Chris Eubank. (PHOTO: BILLY STICKLAND / INPHO)

Tony Quinn and I let the press into the secret about the 'hypnosis' story which frightened the life out of Eubank. (PHOTO: BILLY STICKLAND / INPHO)

**Honey, I'm home: what happened in Millstreet on
18 March 1994 changed our lives forever.**

Arriving at the Burlington hotel with my children Stevie and Caoimhe, and my sister-in-law Niamh.

Dublin, you're my city: an open-top bus ride through the city centre was something I'd dreamed about since watching Barry McGuigan receive the honour in 1985.

but I appreciate that none of it was personal and I hope you do too.'

As it happened, he had perfectly plausible explanations for everything that had happened in the weeks before I fought Pyatt. Whether I believed him or not was irrelevant.

'I don't care about how we get on personally,' I told him. 'If we end up liking each other, then that's a bonus. But I'm most concerned about making money now and if you're of a similar mind, then we could be very good for each other.'

We agreed to meet after Christmas. The ideal date was 13 January, I suggested, since Sky Sports were flying me over to London for the weekend to commentate on the rematch between Vinnie Pazienza and Roberto Duran. We could talk figures then. In the meantime, he said, he'd have a draft contract drawn up and faxed to me.

A CALL OUT OF THE BLUE

It proved to be the shot in the arm I needed. In the days after Christmas, my condition started to improve. The antibiotics seemed to be doing what antibiotics are supposed to do and I began to feel that one day I would be capable of fighting again.

Knowing that I had a big weekend ahead of me, I took to my bed early on Thursday, 12 January, the day before I was due to fly to London. I was sleeping quite soundly until the telephone on my bedside locker rang shortly before midnight. It was Barry Hearn.

Perhaps it was because I was in a state of semi-consciousness, but the conversation was one of the strangest I've ever had. So strange, in fact, that I thought I might have dreamt it. Barry seemed elusive, not having any particular reason for ringing. He just asked me whether I was still doing my roadwork in Dublin and said he hoped he'd be able to tell me soon about my next fight. Again, it was very vague. Then it dawned on me. My bluff was being called here. He must have got word that I was meeting Warren that weekend and he was trying to draw the information out of me. I didn't tell him anything. We made smalltalk for about five minutes and he finished by telling me that boxing was a strange business and that you could never predict what was going to happen from one day to the next. He hung up, leaving me completely bemused.

It wasn't long before I was put out of my misery. At 8am, the phone woke me again. This time, I let the answering machine do its job. 'Steve, it's Barry,' the voice said after the beep. 'I'm in the office till 11am if you wanna give me a call.'

His tone was different this time. It wasn't exactly brusque, but it was certainly more business-like than it had been the night before. He had to know something, I thought. Perhaps he was going to tell me he was prepared to better Warren's offer. Anyway, I decided I had nothing to hide. Managers had made me offers in the past, offers of fights, offers of contracts. I was just looking after my own interests, as Hearn looked after his.

Expecting a row, I was a little taken aback to find him his usual chirpy self when I called him back. Unusually, the conversation began with the same adage that closed the one the night before, that boxing is a strange, unpredictable business. This time, he wasn't so cryptic. He sounded excited. He went on: 'Now, I've got something I want to say to you, Steve, but I need your assurance that you won't breathe a word of this to no-one.'

If I was intrigued by this, I was astonished by what came next. He explained that Ray Close, who was supposed to fight Eubank in Belfast on 11 February, had failed a routine brain scan and was not going to be able to fight. My name had been put on a shortlist of suggested replacements. He asked whether I was interested in moving up a weight to fight for Eubank's WBO super-middleweight title. While I was more than interested, I was very conscious of sounding overkeen.

'Yeh, I'd fight him all right,' I said rather dispassionately, 'but not for less than £200,000.'

Hearn was surprised at my reaction. Winning this fight could make me one of the richest fighters in the sport. It was my opportunity to leave all my difficulties with making the middleweight limit behind me and to break into a division which featured more prestigious names like Eubank,

Benn, Roy Jones and James Toney. I should have been turning cartwheels around the kitchen when I heard that Eubank was prepared even to consider fighting me. Yet all he got back was this cold demand for money.

'Well,' said Hearn, 'you know Chris's attitude. He don't wanna fight no-one unless he can get them for twenty-five grand. And he don't wanna fight you anyway, you know that?'

I knew it all right and that was the reason I felt in such a good bargaining position. Unimpressive against fighters like Dan Schommer, Mauricio Amaral and my old friend from my amateur days Sam Storey, Eubank had helped win back some of his credibility with a points win over Henry Wharton a few weeks earlier. But I got the impression that Hearn believed that Sky might use the cancellation of the Close fight to pull the plug on the entire deal. They could claim that Eubank had breached the contract by not fighting every six weeks. What Hearn needed, and at short notice, was a very credible replacement who was popular in Belfast. While he talked of a shortlist, I knew that mine was the only name that was ever really on it.

I told Hearn that I was flying to London that afternoon and that we could thrash the whole thing out over the weekend. I did realise that this fight could change my entire life. But I decided that, in view of the experiences I'd had during the past seven months, it was unwise to take anything for granted until I was standing in my corner at the King's Hall in Belfast, watching Eubank leapfrog over the top rope and into the ring. So, I decided it was prudent to go ahead with my meeting with Frank Warren regardless.

When I arrived in London that afternoon, I phoned Warren's office, found myself conversing with his answering machine and left the number of my brother-in-law's house in Hounslow, where I was staying for the weekend. Afterwards, I went for a walk to clear my head and consider my options. I'd faced worse dilemmas than this. The offer from Hearn had strengthened my bargaining position with Warren. And while I had the Warren deal to fall back on, I could afford to be more aggressive in my negotiations for the Eubank fight.

After dinner, I phoned Hearn from a payphone in a restaurant in the West End to find out whether he'd passed on my estimate to Eubank. According to Hearn, Eubank wasn't exactly pleased with my demand for £200,000 and used some very colourful language to describe me. Once Hearn had managed to calm him down, he'd agreed to pay me £150,000 for the fight. But the good news was that Hearn would agree to waive his cut from my purse and said the only money that would have to come out of it was 10% for my trainer, Freddy King. No, I said. Freddy could take £15,000 from the profits on the show. If I took the fight for £150,000, there were to be no cuts. We agreed to meet on Sunday to discuss it further. Before hanging up, he said: 'Steve, if I get this for you, I want to own you forever and a day. Right?'

The following morning, I was up, dressed, washed, shaved and on my way to Sky Studios by 6.30am to do the commentary on the Duran/Pazienza fight. Afterwards, I was picked up by Frank Warren's chauffeur. Chatting on the way, the driver told me that Michael Carruth, the Irish Olympic gold medalist who was now fighting for Warren as a professional, was coming to the house too that day, along with a few of Warren's other Irish boxers. Alarm bells sounded. Obviously, Barry Hearn didn't know about this meeting. Word was bound to slip out, though.

'What, they're all going to be in the house now?' I asked.

'Oh, no,' he said. 'They're all coming out for dinner later on. I'll tell them I was talking to you, yeh?'

'No don't,' I said. 'Listen, this meeting never took place, all right? You never saw me today, I was never in your car and never in Frank's house.'

He laughed. 'Oh, I get it. I won't say a word.'

'Thanks.'

As the car turned into the grounds of Warren's mansion in Essex, I'd already made up my mind that I wanted the fight against Eubank, but would negotiate the best deal I possibly could here just in case it didn't materialise. Warren welcomed me at the door and led me into the lounge, where he introduced me to Ernie Fossey, who was Carruth's trainer.

Despite what had happened between us in the past, I couldn't help but be impressed by Warren. Instead of meeting me in an office, he'd invited me into his home, where he introduced me to his family. Noticing how his children were playing together just as mine do, I was seeing him in a new light. Like me, he was just another family man who worked hard in the toughest business of all to try to provide for the people he loved. In boxing, you tend to have a jaundiced view of promoters, managers and trainers, and of fighters who are in the opposite corner to you. But that morning I was introduced to a very human side of him. The fact that he'd also invited Carruth and a few of his other boxers home for dinner that evening told me that he was a man who could relate to the people who worked for him not only on a employer/employee basis, but as partners and friends. That's uncommon in boxing. Warren was a gentleman.

Chris Eubank's name popped up in our conversation. 'I know,' I said, 'that I'll never earn the money I should earn from boxing until I fight him. I know I can beat him.'

'I think you'd beat him as well,' said Warren, 'but when you fight Eubank, you're not only fighting Eubank.'

'What do you mean?'

'Steve, you're fighting the entire system that surrounds him. If you do get to fight him, watch yourself.' Even then I felt there was something prophetic in what he was saying.

Eventually, we started to discuss business. First of all, I explained that I'd considered the proposed contract he had sent to me and had drawn up my own set of changes and terms, which he read over while I spoke to Fossey. He was reasonably happy with all but one of them – the one which required any boxer who beats me to give me (a) a rematch or (b) 25 percent or £25,000 (whichever was greater) from each of his next four defences. No boxer would fight on those terms, he said. With the cuts they're already paying out to promoters, managers, trainers, sparring partners and the taxman, they'd be fighting for practically nothing if they had to hand over another £25,000 to me.

'Well listen, Frank,' I said, 'I've been around for a long time. Long enough to know that I should only be concerned about me and what I'm earning, and knowing that my family will be secure when I stop fighting.'

So we arrived at a compromise. Warren would pay me a £20,000 signing-on fee for a four-fight deal if I agreed to waive my demands for a rematch if I lost my title.

After agreeing to that, there was just one other matter to settle ancillary rights. There was always a chance that video tapes of my fights would sell in Ireland and in the States one day. Seeing as I was the one going through all of the pain in the ring, I deserved a cut from the profits. Warren and Fossey seemed surprised to find themselves negotiating with a boxer who was prepared to look not only beyond his next fight, but beyond his career too. Warren explained that he receives 50 percent of the profits from such things as video tapes and he'd give me ten percent of that, which was 5 percent of the profits. 'Look, let's not haggle all day, Frank,' I said. 'Give me seven-and-a-half percent and I'm happy.'

He agreed, said we had a deal and put his hand out. Now, a handshake in business can be as legally binding as a signature on a contract and Fossey was there to witness it. 'No, Frank,' I said, 'when I see the offer in writing and when I get my solicitor to look through the contract again, then I'll shake your hand to agree on it. What I will do now is shake your hand to thank you for the cup of coffee.' And we shook hands. Before I left, Fossey suggested that I should take up a career in boxing management when I retired from fighting. 'Well,' I said, 'if I'd been as hard-nosed in my negotiations nine years ago, I'd be retired and living in comfort now, which is why I'm not prepared to be sold short at this stage of my career.'

We said goodbye and Warren had his chauffeur drive me to Romford. Over dinner, I switched my mind to the Eubank fight. Provided Hearn's terms were acceptable to me, I'd already decided to ask Warren to put his deal on hold for the time being. Hearn arrived in his office early in the afternoon and I went up to see him. There were a few matters other than money that had to be discussed. I explained that I wasn't prepared to fight for the super-middleweight title if it meant giving up my middleweight belt. Barry was confident that the WBO wouldn't insist that I relinquished my title beforehand, but said he'd have to talk to them first. He said he'd also have to clear the fight with Sky Sports, but, again, he believed that this was just a formality.

'Yeh, that's fine,' I said. 'But to me, the money is the most important thing we have to work out here today.'

'Well, as I said before, we're talking £150,000, minus '

'Minus nothing, Barry. On the phone, I said £150,000, but that wasn't my bid for openers. That's my bottom line.'

'But it's just £15,000 training expenses, for Freddy '

'Barry, I've just come back from a lay-off because of illness and I've had a relapse. I'd rather be given more time than three weeks to move up the weight and to put on a bit of muscle. To be honest, this fight doesn't appeal to me at all. But the £150,000 in my pocket does.'

'Come on, Steve, it's only £15,000, if you –'

'That's not a lot of money to you or to Freddy, because you're both wealthy men. To me, it is a lot of money. Now, I don't want to haggle. That's what I want for this fight.'

He relented and I signed the contract for the fight. So it was agreed. Only formalities had to be seen to now and Hearn said he'd talk to the WBO and to Sky Television on the Monday and details of the fight would be announced in the same week. Before I left the office, Hearn looked at me and grinned: 'You know he's absolutely contemptuous of you, don't ya?'

'Who?' I asked.

'Eubank. He hates you.'

'Does he? Why, what did I ever do on him?'

'I dunno. But he don't like you much.'

'Oh. Well, it doesn't bother me what he thinks of me. I'm going to beat him anyway.'

'Steve, I want to make this clear to you from the start. I usually lead Eubank out to the ring before he fights. But this time, I want to lead the two of you out.'

This gesture meant a lot to me. Since he moved into boxing, Barry hadn't been able to monopolise the sport as he once had done with snooker. But he was proud of the fact that he promoted Eubank, the most marketable commodity in the sport. He was his showpiece boxer. The flagship of his fleet. 'Look,' I said, 'it doesn't matter to me if I have to come out on my own. You just lead Eubank '

'No, Steve,' he said. 'It matters to me.'

BELFAST BLUES, MILLSTREET NEWS

With the excitement of the weekend, I'd forgotten all about my illness. But then, at the most inopportune moment, I suffered a relapse. All the old symptoms had returned with a vengeance and, by Sunday evening I felt worse than I had in Boston a few weeks earlier. News of the fight broke on Monday and the following day, 17 January, I dragged myself from my sickbed, donned the heaviest chunky sweater I could find in my wardrobe and drove to the Europa hotel in Belfast for the press conference.

The official announcement that Ray Close had been forced to withdraw from his fight with Eubank was made first, before I was called into the room. I really felt for Close, having got to know and like him during the eighteen months I spent at Barney Eastwood's gym in Belfast a few years earlier. This should have been his day. When the announcement was made that I was replacing him, I walked into the room and straight over to him to whisper a few words of condolence in his ear. He smiled and nodded in appreciation.

I sat down and explained how delighted I was to get the opportunity to fight Eubank, how I saw it as a turning point in my career and how I wasn't going to be denied this time. To be honest, though, while everyone in the room seemed excited about it, I found it difficult to summon up any kind of enthusiasm about the fight. On the drive back to Dublin, I thought long and hard about what I was doing. The fight was just three weeks away. It was almost six weeks since I'd worn a pair of boxing gloves. I was still very ill and hardly had the stamina to stay awake for more than five or six hours, never mind spend three or four in a gym, building up the extra strength and muscle I'd need against Eubank. The doubts continued in my mind over the next two days until I finally decided that I'd have to ring Hearn and tell him I couldn't go ahead with it.

Only once in my whole life have I got into a boxing ring knowing that I was less than a hundred per cent fit. It was back in my amateur days. One Friday night in January 1985 I was due to fight Belfast's Sam Storey for the Irish middleweight title at the National Stadium. I'd had a bad 'flu for over a week, but wouldn't consider pulling out, frightened that people might say I bottled it if I did. Besides, I was quite sure that a half-fit Steve Collins was capable of winning the title. As it turned out, I was wrong. Storey beat me that night. But when I tried to tell people that I wasn't fit to fight, they just dismissed it as sour grapes. Storey turned professional shortly afterwards and, though I went on to become Irish middleweight champion myself the following year, people said I'd only won it because he wasn't around. That hurt.

Eventually, I did get a chance to avenge my defeat. In March 1988, three years after our last meeting as amateurs, we came face-to-face in Boston, this time as professionals, and this time as equals. Second time around, I beat him convincingly. I was very fortunate to get the opportunity to prove so many people wrong. It didn't matter whether people thought I was bottling it by refusing to fight Eubank on 11 February. I knew I could beat him, but only if I was one hundred per cent fit. This time, there would be no second chances, no opportunity to avenge the result if I lost. It was just one shot at history.

I phoned Barry on Friday to break the bad news to him. He proved more than a little difficult to pin down, having spent most of the day in meetings with the Sky Sports people about the fight. Late in the afternoon, I finally got hold of him. 'How did the meeting go?' I asked.

'Great. They're really thrilled about it, you know, Steve.'

That wasn't what I wanted to hear. I wanted him to tell me that they had doubts, that they needed a few weeks to mull it over and that they'd come back to us with an answer in a month's time.

'Em ... Barry ... How would they feel about a postponement?'

'A what?'

I explained how I was feeling. I explained about Sam Storey and 1985. I explained that I had no doubt in my mind that I could beat Eubank, but that I needed more time to recover from the virus and to start building my strength up again. Expecting shock and disappointment, I was surprised to find him very sympathetic.

'If you fought and you weren't well,' he said, 'I'd never forgive you, you know that?'

To my relief, he said he'd talk to Sky and the WBO about delaying the fight for a month. But in the days afterwards, I was convinced that the same jinx that had dogged the last five months of my life was about to strike again. Rumours started to circulate that Hearn was now having difficulty persuading Sky to accept me as a stand-in. On the morning of 24 January, the *Star* in Dublin reported that the fight was off. Once the story broke in Dublin, people were desperately trying to contact me. Just as I'd done in Boston, I cut myself off from them and stayed in my room, too depressed and too confused to talk to anyone.

But then, within a couple of days, events had taken another dramatic turn. Despite the rumours, Sky had accepted me as an opponent and had a particular reason for being excited about the fight. The month-long delay would allow them to reschedule the fight for St Patrick's weekend. But there was just one stumbling block. The King's Hall was unavailable for the night of Saturday, 18 March. 'I'll check out the Point Depot in Dublin,' Barry told me on the phone, 'but I think we're going to have to switch the fight to London.'

That would have been such a let-down. Potentially, this was the biggest fight in Irish boxing history. But I knew that there was one man who'd make sure it wasn't lost to England.

'What about Millstreet?'

'What street?'

'Millstreet. It's a village in County Cork.'

'Really?'

'Yeh. They held the Eurovision Song Contest there a couple of years ago. You should talk to Noel C. Duggan.'

'Who?'

Only an Englishman could have asked that question. As soon as Hearn made contact with him, he discovered exactly who Noel C. Duggan was – possibly the only man in the world who was more persuasive than him.

Once Hearn had shown an interest in the venue, he didn't stand a chance. Duggan sent reams of faxes down the line to Romford, photographs of the arena, designs of the proposed seating arrangements, a brief history of the area, tourist brochures and enough paperwork to decorate the walls of Hearn's office two or three times over. Eventually, Hearn disconnected the machine and flew to Cork to find out what all the fuss was about. And once he'd done that, there was no way he could refuse.

'Right, that's final,' he told me when he got back, 'it's Steve Collins *versus* Chris Eubank at the Green Glens Arena, Millstreet, County Cork, on 18 March 1995.'

Never before was I so excited about a fight. There were so many good omens. Having spent nine years travelling the world to box, a world champion was coming to my own backyard to fight me. It was taking place in what I've always regarded as *real* Ireland, with its famously warm hospitality and picture-postcard scenery. And it was happening during the St Patrick's weekend. I felt that something extraordinary was on the cards. It was as though it was fated.

Whether it was my destiny or not, there was so much work to be done. Physically, I was still a mess, with my bunged-up nose, sore head and aching joints. My frame of mind wasn't the best it's ever been either. The financial pressure of having earned no money for almost a year, the disappointments in Hong Kong and Boston, the tension of the Pat Petronelli situation and my inability to shake the virus, had exerted an enormous strain on me.

Then I remembered about Tony Quinn, the Irish hypnotherapist and alternative medicine guru. A few months earlier, in an interview on the

'Late Late Show', I was fascinated to hear him talk about a hypnosis technique he used which allowed people to undergo surgical operations without the use of anaesthetic. I've always believed in the ability of the mind to overcome physical obstacles. In the past, I've fought boxers who were fitter and more talented than me, and I won because I was much better prepared psychologically than they were. There were times when I was in trouble in the ring, when I was in pain, when my legs were weak, but my mental strength kept me upright and carried me on to victory. It's difficult to relate this to experienced trainers without being made to feel like a bit of a charlatan. 'No, Steve,' I'd be told. 'The reason you got through was because you did that extra hour in the gym two weeks before the fight or ran the extra mile on the road every morning.'

What interested me most, though, was the mental exercises Quinn used to help people draw out their true potential. As I switched off the television that night, I wondered whether he could help me develop mine. I had thought about telephoning him right then, but as I was about to go into training for the fight in Boston, I didn't get the opportunity. Towards the end of January, I decided to phone him. When I finally managed to track him down, we had a very interesting hour-long conversation, during which he explained precisely how he could help me.

Everybody has mental powers, he explained. They just need to be properly harnessed. There were various mental exercises that would help me prepare for the fight and he could give me some cassettes which I could listen to during all those idle hours I have to while away waiting for the day of the fight to arrive. 'But put it this way,' he said, 'if your mind is in as good a shape as your body, then we're in business.'

'Actually,' I said, 'don't count on that. My body is in pretty bad shape at the moment.'

I explained about the virus. He said he had some herbal remedies that would help cure me and he'd give me a special high-carbohydrate and high-protein diet to follow to rebuild my strength. I asked whether it would be possible to work more closely with him in the weeks before the fight, whether he could become my full-time psychological trainer.

'Difficult,' he said, 'because I'm going to Florida next week.'

Fortunately, I was going to America too. Herbie Hide, who was also trained by Freddy King, was defending his WBO heavyweight title against Riddick Bowe in Las Vegas the week before I fought Eubank. So Freddy and I would have to go to there to work too. 'I'm going to be in Vegas,' I said. 'Would you take a week or so off if I flew you up from Florida to work with me?'

'Definitely,' he agreed.

In the meantime, he arranged to have some of his cassettes posted to my house.

IT'S ALL ABOUT ROOTS

Most people probably considered it bravado when I said I was certain I was going to beat Eubank. They wondered how I could be so supremely confident of succeeding where forty other fighters had failed before me and whether I was making these bold claims to conceal my fear.

In every opponent, you try to identify a weakness. Most fighters have flaws in their techniques. Pyatt's was his tendency to drop his left hand and leave his jaw exposed when he threw a punch. But many fighters have flaws in their characters too. While Eubank was probably one of the strongest boxers in the world physically, in my opinion he was a weak man in a psychological sense. I've always believed in the importance of being honest with oneself. If you develop pretensions about yourself and impersonate something that you're not, then you are making a judgement about your own worth as a person. Eubank seemed to me to have taken on all the mannerisms and extravagances of England's landed gentry – the country mansion, the fast cars, the expensive clothes, the monocle and cane. I didn't think they were part of some media image that had been manufactured for him. As I saw it, he had taken on this lifestyle out of choice, because he was choosing to be something that he wasn't.

Much as I was looking forward to fighting him, I was just as excited about locking horns with him at the official press conference in February at Dublin's Jury's hotel. Eubank's record at pre-fight press conferences was even more impressive than his record in the ring. He'd attended forty-three, won them all and none was even close. Still too sick to train, I spent the few days before the press conference in bed, which gave me time to decide just how I was going to upstage him.

Whether it was deliberate or not, Eubank always mispronounced my surname as 'Collings' every time he spoke about me. So I decided to make the common error of referring to Eubank as 'Eubanks'. Whenever I was being interviewed about the fight, I made the point of saying things like: 'Well, yeh, I am actually looking forward to meeting Eubanks,' putting a heavy emphasis on the S.

'Emm ... Steve, you do know it's Eubank, don't you?' they'd say. 'With no S.'

'Oh, is that right? Seriously? Well, anyway, as I was saying, this fight against Eubanks is going to be ...'

I wanted to remind him at the press conference that he was putting his title on the line in a foreign country, one which had its own language, customs and heritage. So I planned to address the press conference in Irish. Unfortunately, my knowledge of the language consists of what I can remember from school and the bit I picked up on a few family holidays in the Gaeltacht areas of the west. So the television presenter, Seán Bán Breathnach, who's a good friend, helped me out with a short speech.

Clothes would be vital too. While Eubank would be dressed like an English man-about-town, I'd be the quintessential Irishman. I'd match his Armani suit with the light-brown tweed jacket, fawn-coloured waist-coat and dickie bow that I'd got from the well-known Dublin tailor Louis Copeland. He'd have his monocle and cane. And I'd have my accessories too – a flat cap and a blackthorn stick. I'd arrive in the green Jaguar that I'd bought from my brother-in-law the previous summer. Then, there was my *pièce de resistance*. Remembering a woman I knew who bred Irish wolfhounds, I phoned her the weekend before the press conference and asked whether I could borrow one on Monday.

'Oh, that *is* a good idea,' she said, after I explained my rather unusual reason for wanting it. The meeting point we arranged for the handover of the animal was close to Baggot Street bridge at 1.30 pm, half an hour before the conference was due to start.

Gemma and I waited in the Jag for what must have been an hour. But she was delayed. Gemma kept looking at her watch: 'We should be going now, Steve. It was due to start fifteen minutes ago.'

'No, give it a few more minutes,' I said, glad to have an excuse for not arriving on time. Notoriously late for press conferences himself, Eubank was known to be a bit prickly if he was kept waiting. This was *my* day and I was going to make sure he was the one left hanging around. So we waited in the car, by the Grand Canal, until 1:40, by which time it was obvious that she wasn't going to show. Turning the Jag around, we headed over Baggot Street bridge, along Pembroke Road and straight into Jury's carpark. A handful of photographers was waiting outside.

'Where were you?' someone asked.

'I went to see a woman about a dog.'

'A dog? You know Eubank is threatening to walk out?'

'Is he upset?'

'Very.'

'Good.'

We took the elevator up to the room, where the press conference had already started without me. Hearn made up some excuse about my car getting a puncture to try to pacify Eubank, who had been threatening to pull out not only of the press conference but of the fight as well, because of my 'lack of respect'. Just before I stepped into the room, someone said to me: 'Steve, there's a woman downstairs looking for you.'

'For me?'

'Yeh. Says she's got a dog for you.'

Realising she was late, she had come straight to the hotel with it. 'Tell her to bring it up.'

'No,' he said. 'There's a problem. They don't allow dogs in the hotel.'

Being forty-five minutes late was bad enough. Eubank might not have been as understanding if I'd spent a further forty-five looking for the manager and then trying to talk him into changing his hotel's policy on man's best friend. I went on into the room, where supporters seemed to outnumber journalists by a ratio of around 20/1. There was a loud roar as I walked up to the table at the top of the room, where Eubank was sitting, alongside Hearn and the other officials. As I took my seat, he looked me up and down, appearing to admire my clothes. Delighted to meet him at last, I gave him a warm embrace, before making my way to my seat.

After Hearn invited me to say a few words, I read out the speech that Seán Bán had helped me prepare. It ended with the words: '*Deirim libh anois go mbeidh an bua agam ar Christó MacEubank.*'

The translation was innocuous enough: 'I am saying here today that I am going to beat Chris Eubank.'

But the pronunciation of his name in Irish prompted a burst of laughter and a round of applause. Eubank felt he was being ridiculed. It was as though I'd just cracked a joke and everyone in the room was in on it except him. I continued: 'When Chris Eubank gets into the ring in Millstreet, I want everyone to give him a cheer, because he's doing what a lot of fighters wouldn't do today. He's bringing his world title into his opponent's back garden ...'

Then I told him, as I'd told Pyatt almost a year earlier, regardless of what happened between then and the time of the fight, none of it was personal and, after a handshake, ironically enough, hostilities were officially opened.

There was a hush as Eubank stood up to address the room. He stared ahead of him silently for about ten seconds, looked to his left for another ten, then to his right. He looked down at his hands, which were clasped and he seemed to be studying them, as though what he was about to say was written on the back of his hand. He looked up again, staring blankly in front of him, then to the left and then to the right again. And then he said it: 'Steve gets beat.'

There were quizzical looks on people's faces as they considered what they'd just seen. I realised what Eubank's plan was and I had to admit that it was a brilliant one. He'd hypnotised everyone. His silence had just kept a room full of people who despised him totally engrossed for over a minute. He might as well have been swinging a pocket watch in front of their eyes and telling them: 'You are falling into a trance.'

When he said 'Steve gets beat', it was as though he was clicking his fingers and telling them: 'When I sit down now, you are all going to know that, no matter how much you want Steve to win this fight, you know that there is no way he can.'

I had to take the edge away from him. As he took his seat again, I stood up and pulled a piece of paper from my pocket. At home on the previous Friday, I'd sat at the kitchen table and written the script for the fight, the reason why I was destined to win and Eubank to lose. Gemma had typed it up for me in her mother's house that morning and had had it photocopied twenty or thirty times in the hotel manager's office just after we arrived. As she handed copies to the press, I started to read it aloud:

> '*Chris Eubanks has never lost a professional boxing bout. He is both loved and despised by millions of people. He is famous and wealthy from boxing. Chris Eubanks is becoming tired of it all. He's talking about retirement. If he retires, in my opinion, he will not have greatness ... In order to achieve greatness, which I believe every fighter wants, he has to experience defeat, he has to be able to handle it and return and conquer again. I, Steve Collins, am the person who is going to beat Chris Eubanks. I deserve to be the one to beat him more than anyone else. If Chris Eubanks was to pick anyone who is going to beat him, he would choose me. I'm not only the best opponent he's ever going to meet, but he also knows that I deserve this break ... I know I will win this fight. It's a foregone conclusion.*'

When I finished reading it, I folded it up and put it back in my pocket. I explained that I was due to return to Romford that evening and, before

I went back to Castleknock to pack my bags, I also had to collect an award that the hotel had been due to present to me a few months earlier. 'So I'll just take a couple of questions and then I have to go,' I said.

Angry that I was determining both when the press conference started and ended, Eubank abandoned his silence and said he had a question for me. 'You say that because I'm talking about retirement my heart isn't what it was four, five or six years ago?'

'It's in writing. I've put it all down there on paper for you.'

'I know. Retirement is purely prudent. A fighter who stays on too long, he gets hurt. Basically, my health, or your health, our health should be the most important thing in our lives. If you're not healthy, then basically you're screwed up. So, me wanting to retire, I'm only trying to be sensible for myself and therefore my family.'

He hadn't said anything I could disagree with. But then he turned his attention to my use of the word 'greatness'.

'Greatness is usually the concept of what many fighters want,' he said. 'I basically don't have the desire to be great, to be remembered. My desire is to be wealthy ... If I get this greatness, but I don't end up with money afterwards, then who am I? People will look at me in the street and say he's a sad case. This man gave his all to this business, he's a great man and did great things in the boxing business, but look at him. He can't send his children to the schools to which he would like to send his children. He can't afford to drive a car. He has to get on the bus or walk.'

He seemed to misunderstand my use of the word. I wasn't suggesting that Eubank needed to prove to future generations that he was a great boxer. He still had to prove it to his own generation. Perhaps after all the years he'd spent insulating himself against world-class opponents, he'd forgotten that there is still some correlation between being a great boxer and being a wealthy boxer. While he was was earning millions of pounds by getting much-criticised decisions over weaker opponents, there was a limit to the public's tolerance. Sooner or later, he was going to have to prove his class. Whether he liked it or not, 18 March was going to be the first true test of his greatness.

Reading through the rest of the script, Eubank then picked out the word 'deserve'.

He spoke about it: 'You say that if you were to ask Chris Eubank who he would like to beat him, you would be the person because you have done all of what you've done. You have toiled, you have worked hard, you have worked diligently, you have paid your price to this business. Deserve has nothing to do with it.'

I said: 'The truth and the facts are within that statement ... At this stage now, I'm growing, well, not tired of this press conference, but I've got my day planned and I'll answer questions from the public before I leave.'

Eubank's tone started to change. 'You answer me this question,' he said.

'I don't have to,' I replied. 'Are you asking me or telling me?'

'I'm asking you. I'm not telling you anything. I'm telling you that I'm going to beat you. There's no two ways about that. I'm asking you this question –'

'How are you going to beat me, Chris?' I asked.

'That's not the point,' he answered.

'No, that is the point,' I shouted, as the press conference at last turned the way I wanted it to.

'You worry about your training and I'll worry about mine,' he said.

'I know how I'm going to beat you. You probably don't know how you're going to beat me. Because there's no way you can.'

'Talk to me about deserve,' Eubank said.

'Talk to you about deserve?' I asked.

'You're talking about deserve, that you deserve to win. That has nothing to do with it. Why are people in Africa suffering or dying of famine? Do they deserve that? Don't talk to me about deserve.'

Eubank was taking to his soapbox, as he often did at press conferences. He often took the opportunity to talk about war, world famine, inner city decay, Bosnia or whatever else was the flavour of the month. As far as I was concerned, this was a bit rich. I felt he only paid lip service to his African heritage and that it was inconsistent of him to remind me about the plight of the African people, his people, when he was sitting there, dressed like an English gent.

'We're talking about boxing,' I said.

But he continued to try to draw me into this discussion about Africa and I decided I wasn't going to listen to it anymore. 'We're here to talk about boxing. But if you want to bring Africa into it, you are an African, an Anglo-African, of African descent, right?'

A nervous silence fell, as Eubank looked at me and nodded.

'Well,' I continued, 'why do you deny your African heritage and try to impersonate and behave like an Englishman when you're not? You should be proud of your roots and your people.'

A few people at the back of the room broke the silence with a roar of approval and everyone else cheered. I went on: 'I'm Irish, okay? It's a well-known fact. Everything I do, I try to represent my people. I've no disrespect for the Englishman, Scotsman or the Welshman. But I know my roots and I stick to them. That's something I think you've neglected. Maybe you didn't do it intentionally. But you ignore your roots and you try to be something you're not.'

Caught off guard, Eubank said: 'That would be wrong. Speak to me about deserve.'

'Okay. I've worked hard, prepared hard, trained hard. And I deserve breaks. I've earned breaks which haven't come my way. Blame it on politics, blame it on bad luck, blame it on my inexperience. But I know I deserve a break.'

As another round of applause started, I said I'd take a few questions from the press and then I'd be leaving. Still smarting from my remarks, and realising that I was going to upstage him if I arrived last and left first, Eubank announced that he was getting out before me. In an attempt to calm him down, Barney Eastwood, who was sitting a couple of seats away, asked whether he fancied placing his customary bet on the outcome of the fight. During the build-up to his two fights with Ray Close, Eubank had taken high odds from Eastwood that he'd finish Close early on. This time, Eubank was too enraged to hear Eastwood's challenge. He was standing there, looking indignant, asking a group of people surrounding him: 'Is he saying that because I dress like I do, and because I carry a cane that I am denying my African roots? I'm an Englishman.'

'I'm betting you 20 to 1 this time,' said Eastwood, 'the first round.'

'I ain't having no bets. I'm not in a betting fucking mood. Now this is where it's at, yeh?' Eubank responded.

'You're getting cross now,' said Eastwood.

'Cross? Cross? The worst thing to do with me is to upset me. That what he said today is upsetting me. I have nothing in my head now other ... I ain't playing no games or betting or nothing. This man's getting beat, man. Let me go. Barry, I'm getting out of here, right?'

He was followed out to the elevator by Dublin's Lord Mayor, John Gormley, who asked him whether he was interested in accompanying him on a tour of the city. Eubank's now infamous response was: 'Fuck this city.'

People said to me afterwards: 'Steve, you shouldn't have upset him. He's so angry, he'll really go off and train hard for you now.'

Perhaps Eubank would use this memory of how I'd shown him up to help him get through his gruelling sessions in the gym. I hoped he would, becuase I didn't want to beat a half-fit Chris Eubank. I wanted to beat him at his very best.

For the next week, I couldn't escape talk about what I'd said to him. Every journalist who phoned me seemed intent on finding out, not why I was the man most likely to take his title away from him, but whether or not I really was a racist. I couldn't believe that I was having to explain myself.

Racism, for me, is the belief that certain nations or peoples are superior to others. That wasn't even implicit in what I said. Anyway, some of my closest friends were black, including Silky Jones, who carried the Irish flag into the ring for me before I fought Chris Pyatt. I'd sacrificed the best part of many Christmas days to take part in fun-runs in aid of *Goal*, the Irish charity involved in famine relief in Africa. I'd worn the *Goal* logo on my boots when I fought Danny Morgan in Dublin at the end of

1991 and, in the past, had given them gloves and shorts to raffle to help raise money for the relief effort in countries like Somalia, Ethiopia and Sudan.

That was why it was so difficult for me to sit quietly while Chris Eubank, who dresses and enjoys the flamboyant lifestyle of the English aristocracy, lectured me about famine in Africa. Later that week, when he appeared on the Richard Littlejohn show on Sky Television, he tried to defend himself: 'I'm an Englishman. It's not my fault that your ancestors enslaved my people.'

But why, Littlejohn asked, was he intent on dressing like the very people who had enslaved his ancestors? As far as I'm concerned, he never answered that question satisfactorily.

I went back to London that night and all the untruths had already done the rounds. 'Did you hear what Collins called Eubank?'

'Did you hear what Collins said about the starving people in Africa?'

'Did you hear what Collins thinks of black people?'

Those closest to me never believed the worst. But one person who'd believed all the innuendoes and half-truths was Herbie Hide, who confronted me in the gym the following day. 'What did you say at that press conference, eh?'

'What?' I said, caught unawares.

'You made a racist remark. How can you do that when you've got black friends?'

'Herbie, I didn't say –'

'Listen, I heard –'

'Well, don't believe all you hear.' I explained exactly what I'd said.

'That's different,' he said. 'I thought that –'

'No, you didn't think. Don't go making accusations against me again.'

I needed something to help me unwind. Then I remembered the tapes Tony Quinn had sent me. Lying on my bed, I slipped 'Relaxation With A Purpose' into my walkman and listened. 'Most people are caught up in some form of stress, tension, worries, problems, fears, phobias, complexes, etc. It doesn't even sound good, does it? When you really relax, not only physically, but also mentally, to a deep level, all this begins to dissolve and then you will discover that these, which we call mental toxins, were stifling your self expression, your potential and even your self-healing ability.'

After the introduction to the first tape, I'd been won over. There was so much in it that I could relate to. My mental toxins were my legal and financial worries, my illness and the disappointments of Hong Kong and Boston. But, after the press conference, I began to believe that, for the first time in nine years, things were beginning to turn in my favour.

CHAPTER 9

A Night for Greatness

GO WEST, YOUNG MAN

No matter how many times you listen to Tony Quinn's relaxation tapes, there are occasions when you can't help but blow your top. Back in Romford, counting down the days before we were finally due to leave for Las Vegas, I was told: 'Didn't you hear, Steve, we're not going now?'

'What do you mean, we're not going?'

'Herbie Hide, Freddy King, the whole crew. They're all staying in London instead.'

It was true. Hide would conduct most of his preparations for his world title fight against Riddick Bowe in Romford and then travel to the States a couple of weeks before his fight. This meant that, unless Freddy had somehow managed to master the art of bilocation, I was going to have to cancel my flight and hotel bookings and stay at home, to fit around Hide's plans again.

I was seriously annoyed. I had never wanted to go to Las Vegas in the first place. Once I'd been told that I had to if I wanted to be trained, I decided to grin and bear it. But now, just days before I was due to leave, after I'd booked a return flight and four weeks at the MGM Grand hotel, organised some locally based sparring partners to work with me and talked Tony Quinn into clearing three weeks of his very busy schedule to fly up to Vegas from Florida, I was being told: 'Bad luck, Steve, but there's been a change of plan.'

No, I said, it wasn't bad luck. Obstinate as ever, I decided to go to Vegas alone. Perhaps Matchroom want me to lose this fight, I thought. Eubank rakes in millions of pounds for the company every year. What do I bring in? Given the choice, who would they prefer to see holding that title belt aloft at 11pm on 18 March?

I'd do everything for this fight on my own if necessary. While being without my trainer wasn't the ideal situation for the three weeks before the biggest fight of my life, I was experienced enough to know the routine. Anyway, being away would allow me to focus totally on the fight. I could avoid all the questions about my supposed slur of Eubank and escape all the stories about how hard he was training and how much he was going to make me suffer for what I'd said to him. Away from the distractions of life in Romford, I'd train like I've never trained for any fight before, get myself right, physically and mentally. Knowing that nobody afforded me even the remotest chance of beating Eubank would be my incentive.

There was nobody waiting to meet me when I arrived at Las Vegas airport. So, pushing my trolley outside, I hailed a cab at the rank, loaded my cases into the trunk and asked the driver to bring me to the MGM Grand, which, he informed me during the short drive, was the biggest hotel in the world. Biggest or not, I got the 'no room at the inn' treatment when I arrived. For some reason, they had no record of a reservation for me. But I finally got myself checked in and, after nineteen hours of travelling and haggling, was out for the count as soon as my head hit the pillow that night.

As well as being the gambling capital of the world, Las Vegas is also the boxing capital. So, while I hadn't made any prior arrangements for a gym in which to train, the last thing I was going to have difficulty finding there was a ring and some bags to punch. I went straight for the best, the Top Rank gym, which is owned by Bob Arum.

For the next three weeks my room on the eleventh floor of the MGM Grand became a cocoon. A secret password that I'd left at reception protected me from the outside world. The television wasn't switched on once, and I didn't read a single newspaper. Determined to return to Ireland a stronger person in every way, I decided that there was too much negativity in the news. The only people to have access to me during those weeks were my wife and my lawyers, who were keeping me informed of Pat Petronelli's latest attempts to have the breach of contract judgement registered in Britain. Gemma did Trojan work by absorbing all the pressure for me back home, telling me only positive things in her nightly calls to me and turning down repeated requests from my family and friends for the password.

For the first week, I followed the same rituals. Up at 6am for a five-mile run, back to bed for a couple of hours, eat breakfast, relax in my room, listen to tapes, have lunch, go to the gym, shadow box, skip rope, punch bags, spar, go back to the hotel, eat dinner and then, occasionally, do some weight training in the evening-time.

The vibes were good and, physically, I was feeling like a new person by the time Tony Quinn arrived a week later to begin work on my mind. At the outset, we decided to keep his role a secret while we were in Vegas. There was too much nonsense talked about hypnotherapy, too much disinformation. I could envisage the headlines back home: 'Psycho'; 'Collins to fight Eubank in a trance'; 'Dubliner will feel no pain'.

My psychological training would go on behind closed doors. And then, when I won the fight, we'd tell the story of how it was done to a more open-minded audience. So Tony blended in among the holiday makers and the high-rollers, and anyone who did recognise him and made the connection between the two Dubliners was told that we had only met by chance. After a week or so, he checked out of the hotel and rented a house nearby. This made the secret easier to maintain, particularly since a number of sports journalists had started to hang around the hotel. Sitting in the restaurant at night, I'd announce that I was turning in early, make towards the elevator and then slip out the back door unseen and catch a cab down to the house for my sessions in 'the chair'.

Sitting back comfortably, I was told to relax. 'Relax your mind, as well as your body,' Tony said. 'Use all of your senses. Become aware of everything.'

I could hear cars passing on the road outside. There was a fresh smell about the room. I looked around, taking everything in. I became aware of my back touching off the back of the armchair, my elbows on the arms of it, my legs crossed at the ankles in front of me, my heels touching the floor. I was perfectly at peace with myself.

'Now, are you relaxed?' he asked.

'Yes.'

'Good. Now, I want you to remember, Steve, that you could lose this fight to Chris Eubank.'

He watched an expression of horror appear on my face. And he knew that he had got inside my mind.

Until I met Tony, I was, like 99 percent of the world's population, an under-achiever. For years, I believed I was the best middleweight boxer in the world, but on the two biggest nights of my career when I fought Mike McCallum in 1990 and Reggie Johnson in 1992 I couldn't prove it. The memories of these fights haunted me. I'd replayed them so many times in my mind and had no doubt that I'd had the potential to win both of them. But I just couldn't bring it to bear when it mattered most.

I was delighted to discover that I wasn't alone. Tony explained that most people, despite having the potential to realise their ambitions in life, never do. This is because they underestimate themselves. Their conscious mind acts as a barrier, a negative force that tells them that what they want to achieve is just an aspiration and not something that can be attained. Once a person is taught how to take full control of his mind, then his inner potential can be drawn out.

Consider this. Your mind is like a lump of putty that has been allowed to harden. Somebody shows you a way to make it soft and supple again, and while it's like this, uses his fingers to make impressions in it. And when it's allowed to harden again, those impressions don't go away.

The mind is at its most supple when it's in a state of unconscious attention. Like when you're so engrossed in a book that you miss your station on the train. Or so enthralled in a story that someone is telling you that you are not aware of anything else happening around you. Once the mind reaches this state of supreme concentration, Tony explained, it can be programmed in precisely the same way as a computer. The most important programme he wanted to install in my mind was an unshakable belief that I was going to beat Chris Eubank. In order to access my unconscious attention, he asked me to consider the worst-case scenario, that I might lose to him.

Once he said that, I was focused on the fight and its importance. Everything in my life hinged on this, I realised. While I'd still hold the middleweight title if I lost, defeat would damage my marketability in Britain. My future in the ring depended on me winning, as did my family's security. As I considered the enormity of what was at stake, I gave off signals which told Tony that he now had my unconscious attention.

'What will this fight mean to you?' he asked.

'It's a gateway to a new life,' I said. 'I could be a millionaire within a year. I could provide a very good future for my wife and children. For myself personally, I'd go down in history as the first Irishman ever to win two world titles ... I'd make the *Guinness Book of Records* ... Practically every boxer at my weight wants to be the one to beat Chris Eubank. If I did it, I'd be remembered as a great fighter ...'

Once I appreciated exactly what victory would mean to me, he set about persuading me that there was no way that Eubank was going to keep his title on 18 March. Now, he would never have attempted this if he thought I didn't have the ability to beat him or if I really didn't think I was capable myself. Through hypnosis, a man could be convinced that he's a dog. He could get down on all fours, bark and bury bones n the garden all day. But he still wouldn't *be* a dog. As Tony said, he could convince anyone that they could beat Eubank, but that doesn't necessarily mean they could. He doesn't create potential. He merely draws it out.

That is why he performed a psycho-analysis on me when we met first, to satisfy himself that I truly believed I had this potential.

But when he was satisfied, he set about drawing out this inner belief that I was going to win. He asked me to picture Eubank in my mind in various situations. There he was, arriving at the weigh-in, the omnipresent cane in hand, monocle in eye, straddling his Harley Davidson, jodhpurs, riding boots. Then he was jumping over the top rope of a ring with his yellow shorts, white boots, swaggering around the ring in front of me, pouting, preening, dancing like one of The Shadows, looking at me contemptuously, hissing to the crowd: 'I'm gonna beat your man.'

'When you think about him in future,' Tony said, 'it's going to trigger off this feeling in your mind that you are going to beat him.'

When I'd see him, this inner potential would come racing to the surface. I'd associate the sight of him with a very warm sense of confidence in myself and images of me sitting high on people's shoulders, in front of an ecstatic crowd, with Eubank's belt held high in my hands. Whenever I saw him, an overwhelming urge would come over me to tell people what I felt: I'm going to win.

If it had been possible to wish it into reality, Tony's work would have been done after a few days. But saying it over and over again wasn't going to make it happen unless I was physically capable. Tony devised a number of programmes that would help me maximise my athletic ability too.

Sports psychologists have discovered that when a boxer, a tennis player or any athlete who competes as an individual is frightened or intimidated by an opponent, he'll actually see that person as being physically bigger than he really is. So, again, he asked me to picture Eubank, standing opposite me in a ring. 'Reduce him in size,' he said. 'He's getting smaller ... smaller ... smaller.'

And he did, until I towered over him by at least a foot. And when we'd confront one another in the ring, he wouldn't appear as intimidating or as overpowering to me as he had to his previous opponents. We changed his voice, too. We made him speak like Donald Duck, so when I thought of him saying those words 'Steve gets beat', all I heard was this guttural cartoon-voice. Suddenly, in my mind, he wasn't one of the strongest and most revered fighters of his generation any more. He was this five-foot tall Walt Disney character, whom we named 'The Poser'.

Using a similar technique known as 'time distortion', we were also able to make Eubank's punches appear to be three times slower than they actually were. When you're in a state of unconscious attention, your reactions are much faster anyway and I would see shots he threw at me much quicker than I normally would. We also increased the target areas. Parts of Eubank's head and body that were exposed would seem three times bigger than they actually were, making it appear that he was easier to hit. And when I got hit by a punch, my automatic response would be to throw two punches back.

Another evening, Tony said he wanted me to delve into my past and pick out the peak moments in my career, the happiest times I've ever experienced as a professional boxer. Three stood out for me. There was the elation I felt in 1989, when, after the most tense five minutes of my life, an emcee in Atlantic City announced that I'd outpointed Kevin Watts to become the US middleweight champion. There was the feeling of exhilaration I got a year later when I battered Firmin Chirino to defeat in my comeback fight after my first world title defeat. And then there was that incredible moment of weightlessness a year earlier, the night a referee stepped in between me and Chris Pyatt and I was a world champion at last.

Tony told me to close my eyes and to relive the emotions I felt on each of those occasions in turn. He could programme my mind, he explained, so the same rush of adrenalin could be recalled at any given time by performing a simple action, like banging my gloves together. This was known as an 'anchor'. If there was any moment in the ring when I felt tired, this sudden charge of emotion would give me energy. If I felt frustrated, it would offer me hope. If I felt doubtful, it would give me stability and security. After a couple of weeks with Tony, I was convinced that there was no way I could lose. I felt indestructible.

While avoiding newspapers and refusing to watch television in Vegas allowed me to escape all the negativity the news holds, one story I couldn't avoid hearing about was the latest boxing tragedy in Britain. The American boxer Gerald McClellan was in a coma and undergoing an operation to save his life at a hospital in London, after losing a fight to Nigel Benn. Apparently, the fight had been an out-and-out war, with both boxers struggling to find the strength to raise their hands towards the end. Then McClellan, blinking heavily, went down, was counted out while on one knee and then collapsed in his corner, as Benn was declared the winner.

All boxers live with the presence of death. The possibility that every time they step into a ring, they could be shortening their lives or the lives of their opponents. I could make a very facile defence of boxing by quoting the higher fatality rates in other sports, like horse-racing, rugby and motorsports. But to do that, I'd be ignoring the fact that boxing is a very hazardous business. The more you dismiss the dangers, the greater your chances of sustaining long term head injuries. But if you appreciate the risks, then you can minimise them.

I don't take the kind of sustained punishment to the head that almost killed McClellan that night. Unlike him, I have a good defence. While he relied on his ability to take heavy shots and still have the strength to fire back, I rely on my skills to avoid being hit. So the chances of my being seriously injured in the ring are minimal.

However, I didn't need to be reminded that, just a year earlier, I'd been offered the chance to fight McClellan myself. The thought did occur to me that I might have been the one saying prayers at his hospital bedside and wrestling with my conscience over whether it was right to continue fighting. Fate works in strange ways. Later on, it dawned on me that I'd come even closer to fighting the victim of the last major tragedy in boxing, Michael Watson. We were supposed to meet in the spring of 1991, but the fight fell through. He went on to fight Chris Eubank instead, lost on a controversial points decision and then finished the now-infamous rematch in a coma, fighting for his life. I thank God that I didn't fight either Watson or McClellan. In all honesty, I can't say what my attitude to boxing would be if I had been the one who'd delivered those fateful blows. Perhaps I'd want to quit. I don't know. But if I spent time worrying about eventualities, I couldn't bring myself to hit any opponent. While my wife is as mindful of the risks as I am, I was very annoyed to discover that journalists were phoning her in Dublin and asking whether she was frightened for my life, in the light of this recent tragedy. Gemma was at home, trying to cope with the job of rearing three children on her own. The last thing she needed was to be reminded that Michael Watson was in a wheelchair and that I could end up the same way. Or that I might be fighting for survival in an operating theatre by 19 March. Or that I might not be as lucky as that. I thought it was disgusting. Yet she was so tough. When I got home from Vegas, someone gave me a recording of an interview that Joe Duffy had done with her on the 'Gay Byrne Show' and she sounded so strong and so able for his questions.

POWER TO MY PUNCHES

People who've been involved in the business of boxing as long as Freddy King tend to dismiss unconventional training methods as nothing more than fads. They'll tell you that there's no quick and easy way to success. Graft, and graft alone, is what gets you to the top. I didn't quite know how Freddy was going to react when he arrived in Vegas to discover that I had employed a psychological trainer to help me prepare for my fight with 'The Poser'. He was a proud man and I was worried that his nose might be put out of joint. So Tony agreed to give him a wide berth for a few days and to steer clear of the gym until Freddy had adjusted to the idea that I was having my mind trained these days as well as my body.

Once he saw the improvement in my performance, he wasn't sceptical at all. He opened his mind, even to Tony's suggestion that he could eliminate a career's worth of basic errors in my technique in a couple of days. Perhaps it was due to my long lay-off from the ring, but I had unwittingly slipped back into my old habit of dragging my feet when I threw my punches, instead of anchoring them in the way Freddy had shown me. While Tony knew little about boxing, he had a lot of experience in karate, and knew as soon as he saw me sparring that I wasn't getting my full body weight behind my punches. It was a problem with my footwork, I explained, and one which I thought Freddy had managed to coach out of me. Some basic mind exercises could help me to correct it, he suggested.

Freddy, beginning to despair in the same way that other good coaches had before him, agreed to go along with whatever Tony wanted him to do. One evening, we all went out to the house together and Tony took out a video camera. As he dropped a cassette into it and pointed it at Freddy, he asked him to take up a basic boxing stance and then, in frames, show the textbook way to throw a punch. Now, the mind has a photographic memory when it's in a state of unconscious attention. As Tony played the various stages back for me, he asked me to become aware just how it felt to throw a punch in this way, how it looked in each stage. How it felt to stand in the way Freddy was on the video. How the punch sounded as it impacted. And each of the frames was installed in my mind, so that when I went to take up a stance or to throw a punch, my brain sent subliminal messages to my body to tell me just how it should be done. Again, Freddy was astounded at the improvement.

We worked too on countering the psychological effect of Eubank's usual entrance into the ring. It was always brilliantly choreographed. The first notes of Tina Turner's song 'Simply The Best' would sound out over the Tannoy as he appeared in a puff of smoke and then swagger arrogantly towards the ring. He'd stand on the side of it for a minute, looking around, surveying the crowd and then, when he was ready, he'd leapfrog over the top rope, before performing a little shuffle. It was so rousing. Watching it on television, you felt goosebumps and the hairs on your neck stand on end, regardless of what you thought about him. For his opponents, it was such an intimidating ritual.

'It gives him a psychological edge,' I explained to Tony in the house one evening. 'It undermines opponents and gets the crowd on his side.'

He thought for a minute. 'What music are you going to have played coming out to the ring?'

'Well, I usually go for music with an Irish theme,' I said.

'But is there one single tune that really excites you, gets you ready to fight?'

Since I was a child, 'Gonna Fly', the theme tune from the film *Rocky* always got me fired up. Seeing Sylvester Stallone running through that Philadelphia scrapyard, past the markets, along the waterfront and up all those flights of steps and then throwing his hands up in the air as the music reached a magnificent crescendo, it always made you feel as though you could go the distance with Apollo Creed yourself.

'Have you ever heard the theme tune from *Rocky*?' I asked him.

'You want to come out to that? Good. Now, when you get into the ring on the night of the fight, make sure you bring a Walkman with you. We'll get the music on a cassette and, when 'The Poser' is making his way into the ring, you sit down on your stool in the corner, with your eyes closed, put on your headphones and listen to it.'

ALONE IN THE ENEMY CAMP

I decided to leave the States a few days earlier than planned to give myself time to get over the jetlag. So while Herbie Hide was climbing into the ring in Vegas to face Riddick Bowe, I was touching down at Heathrow. I went to the carousel and collected my luggage. In addition to the three sofa-sized suitcases I'd brought out, it now included a large, leather horse's saddle that I'd treated myself to as a souvenir of Nevada. I piled everything onto a baggage trolley, cleared customs and starting looking out for a familiar face. Nobody was there to collect me. Perhaps I was being paranoid, but this was the second time in four weeks that I'd arrived at an airport, jaded tired, to discover that Matchroom hadn't made any arrangements for me. Maybe they didn't get the message that I was coming home early. Still, I couldn't imagine Chris Eubank flying into some city a week before a big fight and being expected to load his bags into the back of a black cab. There'd be a chauffeur waiting for him and he'd be rushed off to some swanky £500-a-night hotel.

After arriving in Romford, I checked into a bed and breakfast, not wishing to return to the house where I was far too accessible. I needed to be alone, to gather my thoughts about the fight, about Eubank, about myself.

The following morning, I heard the news that Hide had lost his world title to Bowe. The pecking order had changed. Now, I was Matchroom's number two. When I beat Eubank the following weekend, I thought, things would change even more.

The following Tuesday, four days before the fight, Freddy arrived back at the gym in Romford to help me wind down my preparations. It was then that he began to appreciate the enormous improvements I had made. Everyone in the gym noticed that my strength and accuracy had improved. My old friend Silky Jones sussed it first. 'It's as though you went over to Vegas and spent two weeks forgetting everything you've ever learned about boxing,' he said, 'and then another two learning the trade again from scratch, except this time better. You're a new fighter and a new man.'

'Silky, you're a wise man, you know that?' I said.

'You're gonna beat him, Steve. I know you are,' he answered.

Freddy was unfortunate enough to feel the improvement in my punching power himself. Standing in the middle of the ring with the pads on his hands, he was telling me to throw certain combinations, like 'right to the head, left to the body, right to the body'. And I was throwing them as quickly as he could say them. A little too quickly, it proved on one occasion. 'Right to the body and left to the head,' he shouted as I stomped after him. The right, thrown straight, sent his hand crashing into his ribs. The left that followed it hit his left pad so hard that it brought his arm right back and almost dislocated his shoulder.

'Arghh!'

'Oh, no, I'm really sorry,' I said, as he bent over, howling in pain.

''Ave you got the facking needle or sumfink?'

'I'm sorry, Freddy.'

'That's ... all right, Steve ... God, you're hitting hard.'

It was fortunate that it was our last training session together. The following day, Thursday, I caught my flight from Stansted to Cork, where the excitement about the fight was already beginning to mount. For the first time in over a month, I read a newspaper on the flight over, turning immediately to the sports section, which featured three pages on the fight. Arriving at Cork Airport, I didn't make the mistake of loitering around the Arrivals lounge to see whether anyone had come to meet me. Instead, I shared a taxi with two WBO officials, who, like me, were spending the weekend in Killarney. Unlike me, however, they were staying at the Aghadoe Heights hotel. To my dismay, I discovered that so too were Eubank, Barry Hearn, the Matchroom team, all of the officials and the three judges. I'd been booked into the Great Southern hotel down the road, along with Freddy King, who wasn't due to arrive in Ireland until the day before the fight. Sitting in my room that night, I felt totally alienated, as though I was the enemy.

While I started to believe that everyone up in the Aghadoe was rooting for Eubank, I consoled myself with the thought that I would be fighting only one man on Saturday night. Lying on my bed that evening, thinking about the fight, my concentration was disrupted by loud clanging noises coming from outside. I looked out the window and discovered that my room overlooked the railway station, where a man was loading steel beer kegs onto a train until late in the evening, anxious to get his work finished before the bank holiday weekend began. Peace and quiet was going to be difficult to find, but I didn't really want it at this stage. I was lonely that night and, with only forty-eight hours to go before the fight, I needed to be around friends, people who believed in me, who would give me encouragement. Tony Quinn had just arrived in Ireland for the fight and he and a few of his friends were renting a cottage in a remote townland a few miles outside Killarney. On Friday morning, when I told him about the hotel arrangements, he invited me up to stay with them. As it turned out, it was the ideal setting for me to sit down in total seclusion and focus on the fight.

Before I left the hotel on Friday morning, I decided to make a final check on my weight, with the official weigh-in only a matter of hours away. The Matchroom people, though, had the scales in the Aghadoe. I was forced to improvise. Downstairs in the Great Southern, in a coldroom next to the kitchen, there was a scales that was used to weigh joints of meat. After the manager agreed to let me use it, I stripped off in this small, icy room, jumped on the scales, took the reading and got dressed again before I could develop hypothermia. While I was bang on the 12 stone, 2lb limit, I knew I couldn't rely on the accuracy of the scales. I decided to bring my sweat clothes and a skipping rope to the weigh-in at the arena that night, just in case I had to work off a few extra ounces.

At the safe house that afternoon, I sat down with Tony and considered how I could get 'The Poser' as upset at the weigh-in that evening as he had been at the press conference six weeks earlier. He had a very good suggestion. He could let it slip that he'd hypnotised me, that I wouldn't feel pain and would keep coming towards him, no matter what was thrown at me. Eubank, who was outwardly so confident, would start to have doubts and begin to question his ability to win.

During the afternoon, we performed some mental exercises together which helped me switch into this very intense, positive frame of mind. Later that night, I watched myself on television, as I stepped from the car, pushed through the crowds and into the Green Glens Arena for the weigh-in. And it excited me. I wore this blank gaze, the fixed stare of a man who was out for what he wanted at any cost. There appeared to be an aura about me. Friends who'd turned up to wish me luck all used the same words to describe me afterwards: like a man possessed. It was as though I was in a trance, they said. The reverse was actually the case, though. I felt more in control of myself than at any other stage in my life.

THE WEIGH-IN

While the weigh-in will probably always stand out in the memory of the three or four thousand people who turned up to watch it, it very nearly didn't happen at all. We set off in good time early in the evening, but hit one of the biggest traffic jams I've ever seen on the approach to Millstreet. The local St Patrick's Day parade had caused an enormous tailback and, sitting in the back of the car, I wondered whether Eubank was already at the arena and whether he was threatening to pull out of the fight, just as he had when I arrived late to the press conference. After waiting for about twenty minutes for the traffic to start crawling forward again, I suggested getting out of the jam and driving on the opposite side of the road.

'We'll get arrested,' said Tony.

'No,' I said. 'They'll understand. Special circumstances and all that.'

So he turned the wheel of the car right and we drove for a mile and a half on the wrong side of the road, past all these hundreds of cars, sounding our horn. As we drove by, all the other frustrated motorists began to realise who we were and they started beeping theirs too. At a junction at the top of the road, there was a Garda roadblock.

'The police,' said Tony. 'What will we say?'

'Leave it to me,' I said, getting out of the car.

I walked up to the officer in charge. 'How are you? I'm really sorry, but I'm Steve Collins and I'm fighting in Millstreet tomorrow and I'm supposed to be at the weigh-in already. I had to drive on the wrong side of the road to get up here and I'm really sorry for that, but if I don't get ...'

Of course, he knew all about the fight. He called over one of his colleagues, a motorcycle Garda. 'Give Steve an escort down to the Green Glens and make sure he gets there on time.'

The official weigh-in was due to take place in the ring. But Mel Christle, the president of the Boxing Union of Ireland, objected, pointing out that an accurate reading could only be obtained if the scales were set on a solid floor. The doors of the arena had been opened to the public and more than three thousand people were inside, waiting to see us climb through the ropes and have our weight checked. Eventually, a compromise was hammered out. The official weigh-in would take place upstairs, unknown to the crowds. Then, once Mel was satisfied that we were both on or below the super-middleweight limit, the scales could be brought downstairs and we could go through the motions of weighing in a second time for the benefit of the people and the television cameras.

This actually suited me. The meat scales back in the hotel kitchen obviously weren't quite as sophisticated as the scales at the arena. While I was quite prepared for the fact I was slightly over the limit, I didn't want to have to be told, in front of those three thousand people, that I'd have to go back to the gym and sweat off a few ounces. It was better that it happened backstage.

Just as I expected, I found myself a quarter of a pound over the limit, much to the amusement of Eubank, who looked at me and sneered. I went out to the toilet, but couldn't go. Opening my gear-bag, I took out my rope and started to skip to try to take the extra ounces off. After a minute or so, Eubank came over to where I was working, looked me up and down and smiled. 'Ah, Collings,' he said, rather smugly. 'This is very unprofessional, isn't it? Trying to lose weight at this late hour.'

The sight of him triggered off this great feeling of confidence in my mind. I stopped skipping, looked directly into his eyes and said: 'I'm going to win.'

He seemed a little uneasy. As I started jumping the rope again, he walked over to the other side of the room, where he started to ridicule Freddy King, who had once worked with him. 'This is most unprofessional. Your man is having difficulty making the weight. I thought he was an experienced fighter. He isn't even ready for the fight.'

As Freddy started to give me a body rub, Eubank continued: 'Listen, when I take care of this guy, Freddy, why don't you come back to me and work with a real champion?'

I turned to Freddy. 'Either tell him to shut up,' I said, 'or I'm going to go over and flatten him.'

But he just smiled at Eubank, humouring him.

A steward came in to announce that the routine medical check was due to take place, so I asked him where we'd have to go.

'Who are you?' he asked. Eubank was just behind me.

'He's Chris Eubank,' said Freddy King, jokingly.

'I'm Steve Collins,' I said.

'Oh, listen, I'm very, very sorry,' he said.

Eubank, though, found it very amusing. 'Ha ha,' he said. 'Steve Collings. Even his own countrymen don't recognise him.'

The steward later apologised profusely.

'Don't worry about it,' I said. 'Everyone will know who I am when I beat him tomorrow night. And you'll still be welcome to the celebration party. But you're buying the drink, okay?'

Freddy continued with my rubdown.

'Hey, Freddy,' said Eubank, 'how come you never gave me a rubdown like that when I was working with you, eh?'

So I walked over to him. 'He's giving me a rubdown because I'm going to win.'

'I wasn't talking to you,' he said. 'Don't be so ignorant.'

'I'm being ignorant because I'm going to win.'

I pushed my face towards his, until our noses were no more than a couple of inches apart. Looking into his eyes, I gave him a deep, almost maniacal stare. 'I'm going to win,' I said. 'I'm going to win. I'm going to win. I'm going to win.'

He swallowed hard. He looked seriously rattled, as though he'd just discovered that the biggest enemy in his life at that moment was not only the most self-assured man he'd ever met, but was deranged as well. As I walked away, he turned to his trainer, Ronnie Davies. 'He seems very confident,' he was overhead to say. 'I was never that confident before a fight.'

'Don't worry about it, Chris, he's all hyped up, that's all.'

'I have never been that confident before a fight,' Eubank said again.

'It's like he's mad or something, isn't it?' said Davies.

'I have never ever been that confident.'

'Maybe he's hypnotised.'

Tony, who was standing beside them as this conversation was going on, decided to germinate the seeds of doubt in Eubank's mind. 'It might very well be hypnosis,' he said aloud, as Eubank and Davis spun around and looked him up and down, wondering who he was and why he spoke with such authority.

'Hypnosis?' Eubank said with an alarmed look on his face. 'He's hypnotised. No, this is not right.'

Meanwhile, a couple of English journalists, sensing that I wasn't the same Steve Collins they'd met so many times before, said: 'Steve, it's not like you at all. It's like you're out of control or something. What's happened to you?'

'If you want to know that, you'll have to speak to that man there,' I said, pointing at Tony.

They turned to him. 'Who are you?' he was asked.

'Well, my name is Tony Quinn and I'm a doctor of clinical hypnosis and I've been working with Steve for the past month.'

Noticing that Eubank was eavesdropping on this, he started to embellish the story. 'When Eubank hits him, I've ensured that Steve will not feel any pain. He'll find Eubank very easy to hit. He'll also be able to punch harder himself.'

As I stepped back on the scales and made the weight at the second attempt, Eubank's mind was troubled. Here was an opponent who wasn't going to feel a thing. He thought I'd just keep coming at him, no matter how many punches he threw at me. He looked a little dazed as I was ushered down the stairs, through the crowd and into the ring for the second weigh-in. My expression was blank, my eyes vacant and my mind focused as I climbed through the ropes and waited for Eubank to arrive. When he did, I made a beeline for him and said into his ear: 'I'm going to win.'

Visibly distressed, he turned his back on me and walked over to the other side of the ring. I followed him, trying to make eye contact with him and told him again: 'I'm going to win.'

He turned his back on me a second time and pushed backwards against me. I gave him a shove and he staggered forward, while Barry Hearn stepped in between us to prevent the fight starting twenty-four hours early. I was called to the scales and held my hands aloft as Mel Christle read out the weight that had been taken at the official weigh-in upstairs.

As I was leaving, Eubank was making loud protests to anyone who cared to listen. 'Steve Collings has been hypnotised,' he said. 'This is not right. How can I fight a man who has been hypnotised? He will not feel pain. This is dangerous. It is wrong.'

On the drive back to the safe house, we rolled around with laughter. 'We've fooled him,' I told Tony. 'We've fooled "The Poser".'

'He's frightened, you know that?'

'For the first time in my life, I've seen Chris Eubank frightened. I have him. I know it. I won the press conference. I won the weigh-in. The final round is tomorrow. I'll win the fight.'

TOUGH GUYS DON'T DANCE

How to beat Chris Eubank was a question that had occupied the minds of forty-three fighters before me, but none was as well equipped to win as I was. Freddy King's advice to me had been to box cautiously, to keep moving, let Eubank pursue me and keep picking him off with my jab while on the retreat. But I'd seen too many other boxers adopt this tactic against him and lose, with the judges always seeming to reward Eubank rather over-generously for his aggression in coming forward. Instead, I was going to dictate the fight, control it from the first bell and beat him decisively, leaving no room for the judges to doubt who had won.

Few people believed I would beat Eubank because few people knew much about me. But those who'd followed my career in the United States knew that Eubank's style was the perfect foil for mine. He liked to fight in spurts, to take a step backwards, assess his last move, contemplate his next, strike a pose to incite the crowd, throw a long and lazy jab, drop his hands and embark on a bit of a walk, then come back and fight some more. I liked to come forward, to stalk opponents who stood off, throw flurries of punches, take a couple back, wrestle my way out of clinches, keeping my jab busy until there was an opportunity to throw a hook, but all the time coming forward relentlessly.

He wouldn't be afforded the luxury of boxing for forty-five seconds of every round. It would be a long and tortuous fight, during which he'd have to dig deep into his reserves of strength and stamina to keep fighting until the final bell.

It was still a fight that would be won by the man who was in better psychic condition. And while I knew that Eubank was frightened as I left the arena after the weigh-in, I didn't appreciate just how frightened until Tony gave me the newspapers on the morning of the fight. He'd refused to leave the arena for two hours and, until Barry Hearn talked him around, he was adamant that he was not going ahead with the fight. 'I'm afraid,' he told a reporter from Sky News. 'I'm entering unknown territory. I don't know what I'm dealing with. I shouldn't be in that ring. I'm fighting a man who is mechanically orientated ...'

All boxers share those fears, but I was astonished that Eubank had voiced his. It's a cardinal rule of boxing that you never admit when you're frightened, certainly not to an opponent and particularly not to yourself. Had I discovered that he'd been using a hypnotist, I'd have thought: Damn, he's got an advantage over me, but he still has one hell of a fight on his hands.

On the afternoon of the fight, one of Tony's friends phoned John Wishausen, who works with Matchroom, to find out what time I was due to be at the arena. It turned out that they'd been making frantic efforts to contact me all day. There was promotional work to be done, journalists wanted to talk to me, Sky Sports needed to interview me, and I seemed to have just disappeared off the face of the earth.

'Where is Steve now?' John asked Tony's friend.

'I can't tell you that,' she answered. 'Just tell me what time he's due to be at the arena tonight.'

'This is important. We need to talk to him. Where have you got him?' he said, sounding as though he believed I'd be abducted by some strange cult.

'I've already told you,' she insisted. 'He doesn't want to talk to anyone. Now, he wants to arrive at about eight o'clock. So, I'll tell you what. Have the Garda escort waiting in the town for him at around seven-thirty.'

I arrived through the front doors of the Green Glens Arena with a cordon of Gardaí around me and was led up the two flights of wooden stairs to the room where the weigh-in had taken place the night before. But this time, there seemed to have been an astonishing oversight on someone's part. There didn't appear to be a dressing-room for me. Eubank had his. It was straight through the function room and at the first turn to the right. We wandered around for about five minutes, repeatedly asking people where I was supposed to change, until finally I was led into a long room, which looked as though it had been set up for a board meeting. In the middle of the floor stood a table and six chairs. While it was unconventional to say the least, I didn't bother wasting my energy arguing. I just got on with my usual pre-fight rituals, checking my gear, taking out my boots, mouthpiece, grease, foul protector and the new shorts and gown I'd had made. While I was doing this, Tony was talking to me, being positive, reminding me of all the exercises we'd done over the previous few weeks. I'd left word with the Gardaí who were on the door that no-one was to be allowed into the room, except Freddy and Jason King and Tony Quinn, as well as George Patrick, who would be giving them assistance in my corner. No brothers, no cousins, no friends, no long-lost relatives were to be allowed near me until after the fight.

I was very switched on, so completely focused that I hardly heard the loud rap on the door from a television crew who wanted to interview me for Sky Sports. Eventually, I was persuaded to allow them in for a very brief interview. When they'd set up the camera, the reporter, Gary Norman, was given his instructions to start. 'Steve,' he said, 'I know you very well and I've never seen you this intense.'

'Basically,' I said, 'I'm prepared for this fight better than I've prepared ever before. Not only physically but mentally.'

'And what do you think's gonna happen?'

'I'm going to win,' I said, before turning my head to the camera. 'New champ.'

I turned my back and walked away. As the crew left, Mel Christle of the Boxing Union of Ireland arrived at the door and explained the usual pre-fight procedures to me. Two people would have to observe me having my hands bandaged before my gloves were put on. One would be an official from the BUI. The other would be a member of Eubank's entourage. But, with only half an hour to go to fight time, I suspected that Eubank might send in someone with the intention of upsetting me.

'Who is coming in for him?' I asked.

'I don't know,' Mel said.

'Well, listen, if I don't like him, I'm throwing him out. All right?'

As it turned out, his observer was his friend, Maximo Prerrett, a Puerto Rican-born New Yorker, who was on his best behaviour when he came in. He sat silently and watched as Freddy wound the bandages around my hands and taped them. Before he left, he shook hands with Freddy and then offered me a handshake. 'No,' I said. 'Business.'

He nodded and, as he turned towards the door, I called out to him.

'*Si?*' he said.

'*Comprende Inglés?*'

'*Si.*'

'I'm going to win.'

Barry Hearn came in to see me, looking a shade concerned. While he'd offered to lead me out to the ring a few weeks earlier, there now appeared to be logistical problems. It would have meant walking up to the ring with me, climbing in, climbing out again, walking back through the crowds to Eubank's dressing-room and then walking down to the ring again. Sky Sports had a fairly rigid schedule they had to adhere to and it just wouldn't have been possible. I told him that I didn't mind. He always led Eubank out and I wouldn't consider it disloyalty if he did it this time.

'Em ... Barney Eastwood wants to know can he lead you out,' he asked.

I was more than happy with this. Eastwood, who was co-promoting the event, had been my manager for almost two years after I returned from America in 1991. He'd helped give my career direction and a new impetus at a time when I was very disillusioned with the sport and we'd remained good friends since our contract expired and I moved to Hearn's camp.

'Yeh, tell Barney I'd love him to do it.'

'Listen, best of luck to you, Steve,' Barry said.

'Thanks.'

He left. After Freddy and my seconds gave me my final instructions, I gave them theirs. Between rounds, I wanted Freddy to get into the ring to my right and for Tony Quinn to talk to me from the left. Jason was to hand Freddy the water bottle, slops bucket, grease, iron and whatever else he needed through the ropes. 'Under no circumstances,' I said to George Francis, 'is anyone to stop Tony from getting up and standing on the side of the ring.'

My gloves were tied and, as an official stuck his head around the door and told us we had five more minutes, I let out a shout: 'NEW CHAMP.' Tony shouted it too.

Freddy and I did some last-minute padwork to sharpen me up, but the soreness in his ribs and shoulder forced us to abandon it early. 'I'm gonna need a holiday after this,' he joked.

And then the official appeared again and told us it was time to go. My Walkman was clipped onto my shorts and I slipped the robe on. 'Now,' I said to Jason, 'carry the headphones down to the ring and have the stool ready for me as soon as I get in. I'm going to turn it on, sit down and go to sleep. Right?'

Jason looked stunned, but said he'd do it.

We walked out of the dressing-room and there was an entourage of Gardaí waiting to accompany me to the ring, which really pleased me. There were no butterflies or weak knees as we walked down the stairs. No goosebumps as the emcee announced my name and I was greeted at the entrance to the arena by this loud cacophony of noise. Hood up and head down, I stood in the darkness at the top of the aisle and waited for the music to start. Suddenly, this enormous fog of dry ice started to ascend from the floor and I had to take a few steps backwards. The idea was that I'd appear in a big puff of smoke, as the music started, but the stuff was choking me. As the first notes of 'Gonna Fly' sounded out over the

Tannoy, I waited for the smoke to clear and then we started to shuffle towards the ring. Recognising the tune immediately, the audience became excited. This was new to me. On the few occasions when I'd experienced a reception like it, is was always for the other guy. But I knew there was something very intoxicating about it, and that in savouring it I might somehow forget that it was I and not this partisan crowd who was fighting Eubank. I just kept my eyes on the floor and was nodding my head, mouthing the words that I'd been reciting like a prayer from the very first day I met Tony Quinn in Vegas: 'I'm going to win ... I'm going to win ... New champ ... Steve Collins, new champ.'

A DATE WITH DESTINY

It seemed like no distance at all to the ring. My brother, Mick, jumped up on the side, pulled open the ropes and I climbed through. I held my hands aloft and gave a smile which seemed to show that I knew this was my date with destiny. I punched my gloves together as Tony had taught me and this great tide of exhilaration came over me. I closed my eyes as the noise increased a few more decibels and filled my lungs with air as if to suck this incredible atmosphere in and feed off it. Jason produced the Walkman, fitted it onto my ears and Tony zipped up my gown and pulled up my hood again. Freddy put the stool under me and I sat down to relax and listen to the tape. While it was on at full volume, it would have been impossible not to hear the loud strains of 'Steve-oh' and *Olé, Olé, Olé*. Neither could it drown out the voice of the emcee, as he introduced Eubank and over the Tannoy came this tune, the kind of orchestral arrangement that often signals the appearance of a villain in a film or a play.

I wasn't aware that Eubank was sitting astride a £10,000 Harley Davidson and was being hoisted up, high above the arena, from where he was looking down on the crowd disdainfully. But I did hear Tina Turner's voice shortly afterwards: 'I call you ... when I need you ... and my heart's on fire ...'

It didn't matter that I heard it, as long as Eubank didn't think I did. I wish I could have seen through my shut eyelids to catch his reaction as he vaulted the top rope and discovered that I'd missed his entrance. As he caught sight of me, sitting impassively in the corner, with my head up, my eyes closed and the headphones on, the curiosity must have been killing him. He must have wondered was 'Steve Collings' being hypnotised in his corner?

As we were both being introduced, the Rocky theme tune in my Walkman was reaching its dramatic end. I waited for about another minute before opening my eyes. Having had them closed for the best part of ten minutes, it took a few seconds for them to adjust, as if I'd just been woken from a deep sleep by the switching on of a light. I looked across at Eubank for the first time and he was staring at me. Tony pulled the headphones off my ears and Freddy peeled off my jacket, as I lifted myself from the stool. I punched my gloves together again while the referee, Ron Lipton, motioned me towards the centre of the ring, where Eubank was already waiting for our instructions.

Glowering at him, I said: 'I'm going to kill you,' and the referee felt obliged to tell us: 'I want you to remain professional at all times.'

Ronnie Davies, obviously sharing the concerns that Eubank had expressed the previous night, did something I've never seen a trainer do before. He stood between us, with his back half-turned away from me and his arm outstretched to keep me away, as though he was terrified that I was so out of control I might throw a punch at his man before the bout had even started. Eubank refused to look at me, but I talked to him incessantly as the referee completed his instructions. 'I'm going to win,' I muttered. 'I'm going to win. I'm going to win ...'

We turned to our corners for the last time and the first bell sounded.

Round One: Sometimes the first round of a fight can be the fight itself. Patterns can be determined early on. There are times when you know, as early as the third minute, that you're strong enough to knock your opponent out, or that he's going to try to outbox you and tire you, or that no punch you throw is going to trouble him. So it was with this fight. For every punch Eubank aimed at me, my immediate response was to throw two back. I'd fire them off in quick succession, without being fully aware of how many I was going to throw until the punches had actually left my shoulder. The opening minute or so was tentative. I seized the initiative midway through the round, opening up on him with both hands, before he managed to manoeuvre himself out of trouble with two left jabs. He moved inside my guard and landed a punch. But he found two in his face and I'd stepped back again, out of his range, while he was still shaping up to throw another. Early on, he seemed to anticipate that my counter-punching was going to cause him problems and he chose to jab his way through the rest of the round, while I continued to pursue him and hit him at will until the bell sounded. As he strutted back to his corner, he realised if he didn't know before that he was in for the most torrid night of his career.

Round Two: This realisation probably explains his urgency at the beginning of the second round, when he charged straight across the ring and hit me with two shots to the body and a third to the head. I threw a combination of punches back at him, but, caught off balance, I fell to one knee. While Eubank claimed he had put me down, I was back on my feet at once, and the referee agreed that I'd slipped. He waved us on and Eubank hit me with another left jab, before adopting a 'peek-a-boo' stance, holding his gloves up to his temples and inviting me to hit him. I managed to get through his guard with surprising ease, though. I drove hard shots into his face with both hands, until he came out of defence to send an uppercut crushing into my body, the first punch that had caused me any real discomfort. Instinctively, I threw back and he leaned away from me as I opened up on him again. Heartened by his success last time, he came inside to try to throw another body shot, but before he got the chance to retreat, he'd been hit two hard punches. His frustration was growing by the time he tried it a third time, and got stung by a combination of three shots. The first two cuffed him about the head, while the last, a left, hit him hard in the side of the face and brought his head crashing to the left. Angry now, he aimed three punches at me, but I opened up with a volley of shots as he covered up on the ropes. Looking a little ragged, Eubank swung a reckless shot which missed and turned him around, as I pounced on him on the ropes, raining punches down on him as he tried to tie my arms in knots and hold on. There was no question that I'd won the round.

Round Three: I was finding it increasingly easier to hit him. Again, he began on the offensive, finding the range with three jabs, before bringing a right crashing across my face. A left to the side of my head and a right, which made a dull thud as it hit my ribs, had me stepping backwards again. As I tried to regain control in those opening seconds, he buried another uppercut into the pit of my stomach. But his first moment of encouragement in the fight didn't last long. As we moved towards the middle of the ring, he was hurt by a solid combination, the left setting him up for a right that snapped his head back. He wasn't as elusive as I'd expected him to be. The target areas did appear bigger, just as Tony said they would. Even when Eubank covered the sides of his head with his gloves, I still managed to drive solid punches through, into his face. At the same time, he was having great difficulty reaching me with everything and his frustration started to show when he tried to engage me in conversation.

'Come on, Steve,' he said, waving me towards him, hoping that I'd stop counter-punching and allow myself to be drawn in, to stand with him and fight toe-to-toe, in a test of power that he thought he'd win. I didn't oblige, preferring to keep scoring with my jab. Annoyed that I hadn't taken the bait, he swung a wild left hook at me, but I had time to duck and the force of the punch spun him around and left him slung over the top rope, facing the crowd. As the round wore on, he tried again to smother my punches by covering his head with his gloves, but I managed to drive a right straight through and hurt him again. It was another round for me.

Round Four: Eubank's best work was again confined to the opening seconds, as he fought his way out of a corner with two punches. But I stepped out of the way, as two more whistled past my body. I smiled and muttered: 'Hard luck, Chris.'

In retaliation, when my next two shots failed narrowly to connect, he shook his head in derision. But the pattern of the early rounds continued, as he attempted to step nimbly inside to try to hit me, but got caught with two hard punches as he wound up to throw his second. My balance failed me again, though, and I felt my legs disappear from under me as I tried to stay out of reach of his jab and crashed against the ropes. I regained my composure quickly and finished the round by again driving three solid shots through his guard and into his face.

Round Five: It had become apparent to me that Eubank thought he could weaken my legs by hurting my body, and my solar plexus was again a target as we fought at close quarters at the beginning of the round. But he still hadn't managed to hurt me with anything. Then he allowed his own defence to lapse. He stood in front of me square on, his hands low, leaning slightly to his right and concentrating on the left-hand side of my face, as though he was so shocked to find an opening that he couldn't take advantage of. Perhaps it was Tony's time-distortion programme at work again, but my reaction was quicker, catching him cold with a left to the face and following it with a hard right to the side of his head. BANG! Seconds later, when I hit him with a short, clubbing right, I sensed, for the first time in the fight that he was in real trouble. As he tried to fight back, he brought his knee up, the action of an increasingly desperate man, and incurred a warning from the referee. Another short right that had all of my body weight behind it sent him back-pedalling and, believing he was in trouble, I didn't allow him a respite. I hit him hard with both hands as he fell wearily against the ropes. Two more left-right combinations had him backing off again and I caught him with a right before the bell sounded. As I returned to my corner, I knew he was hurt and becomingly increasingly frustrated, while I was growing in strength and confidence.

Round Six: Again he sought a fast start but, after hitting me with a good left to the body and a right to the head, he felt the full force of perhaps the heaviest punch of the fight. It rocked his head sideways and was followed by a big right over the top. Keeping well out of his reach now, I taunted him when he lunged forward and made light contact with the back of my head. As he raised a first in triumph, I smiled and tapped the back of my head with my glove to tell him that his effort had been wasted. He shook his head in similar fashion after I managed, again with surprising ease, to crack him across the side of the head. By this time, the signs of tiredness in him were as apparent to me as the signs of frustration. He was breathing more heavily now and retreating towards the end of the round. As he sought sanctuary on the ropes, I unleashed three more hard punches, before he managed to spin around and get himself out of trouble. But, with the fight half over, he must have known that he still hadn't won a round.

Round Seven: As I continued to counter-punch well, he began to have the look of a tired man who had tried everything and didn't know what to do next. I was too quick for him, too elusive, too skilful, too accurate. After receiving a stern rebuke from the referee for hitting me in the face with an elbow, he launched an extraordinary punch that resembled a cricketer's bowling action. I'd slipped well out of its way by the time it had risen up and then suddenly descended from three or four inches above my head to a couple of inches from the ground. He crouched over to protect himself after I hit him with a strong left and we traded punches. When, at last, he found some rhythm towards the middle of the round, he managed to make me look a shade disorganised, finding me consistently with the jab. But he had to survive a difficult moment on the ropes and was in trouble again in the last seconds of the round, staggered by two short punches to either side of his head. As he backed off, visibly hurt, I followed him and landed three more good shots. While he punched the air and swaggered back to his corner, he had the unmistakable look of a man who knew he was going to lose his title.

Round Eight: Eubank finally crumbled. I had become aware of the fact that I was instinctively taking up the textbook boxer's stance when I was coming out for rounds and I was hitting Eubank harder than I'd hit anyone else before. It wouldn't be long, I told myself, before he'd fall. At the beginning of the eighth, he aimed a right hook to my ribs and I bent my body at the waist to absorb it as it came crashing into my side. But I responded with two good punches before Eubank could put any distance between us. Twice more, he went to the body. I threw out a speculative jab, which fell just inches short of his chin, but brought a more deliberate right thudding into his midriff shortly afterwards. Instantly, I knew it had hurt him. Noticing his hands held low, I spotted the opportunity to throw the two-punch combination that had almost ended Freddy King's training career a week earlier. The first punch, the right, hit him straight in the side. WHACK! His shoulders dropped, all of the muscles in his body relaxed and he fell backwards onto the canvas, the impact of the fall lifting his feet high in the air and almost over his head. The left that came after it was a much better punch but, with Eubank already on his way down, it whistled harmlessly over his head. All hell broke loose in the arena, as I walked the two or three steps back to a neutral corner. I remember being a little annoyed that he'd fallen when he had and was certain he wouldn't have recovered from the second punch had it caught him. As it was, he did and he protested loudly that he'd slipped, as he climbed to his feet and the referee picked up the count. Listening as it reached eight, I remembered that, like a wild animal that's cornered, Eubank is at his most dangerous when he's hurt. Who could forget the way he picked himself up off the floor to batter Nigel Benn to defeat? Or against Michael Watson, how he got up from a knockdown that should have finished him and summoned up the strength to deliver an astonishing uppercut that won him the fight and, as it happened, almost cost Watson his life? I remained wary as I moved in on him, seeking to press home my advantage and he bent in half to try to protect his body as I let go with both hands. Two hard punches to the face snapped his head back and he suddenly found himself standing upright and taking three more punches to the head. But, as expected, he suddenly attacked, catching me with a beautiful left to the chin that sent me reeling backwards and onto the ropes. He threw himself at me, trying to tough me up inside and wrestle my arms apart. He threw a right, which I did well to ride, but I knew I had to get off the ropes, where I was at his mercy. I hit him with with a good shot and moved to my right. He followed me and tried to catch me again, but we clashed heads and our arms became entangled. We waltzed each other in a clinch for a few seconds before the bell finally rang. It was a big round for me. The judges would have to score it 10-8. There was no longer any doubt in my mind that, as long as I was standing upright when that final bell rang, I'd win.

Round Nine: Whether it was indignation at being put down or the sudden realisation that he was well behind on points, Eubank was more fired up now. And I was only beginning to appreciate just how strong he was. He seemed to have recovered from the knockdown and he threw a similar combination at me, with a right to my ribs and left to my head. He threw two more shots and I stepped backwards. But then his work looked a bit desperate again. He bowled another over-arm right, which I sidestepped, and he found himself in a corner. This was my opportunity to regain the initiative and I threw a barrage of punches at him. For the first time in the fight, Eubank seemed to realise just how close he was to losing his title. He knew he needed something special. A right found the side of my head, but I rode the punch and stuck my chin out at him, as if to tell him: 'Look, even your best shot can't hurt me.' Obviously angered, he aimed another upper-cut into my stomach, but instinctively I hit him with three punches BANG, BANG, BANG before he could make himself scarce. As he stepped backwards, I pursued him and he leaned away from me, trying in vain to avoid three more solid punches. Feeling the pace now, I punched my gloves together, just as Tony had taught me, and I found a new gear. I started to move again, dancing around Eubank as he stood in the centre of the ring, breathing even more deeply now and looking a bit forlorn. As he crouched down low, looking for an opening in my guard, I managed to crack him with a rather effortless right. I'd won another round and my only concern was that Eubank was going to have to respond now.

Round Ten: Eubank proved his championship class. He had already confirmed what I'd suspected all along during the years he'd spent insulated against world-class opposition – he had lost his edge. It took something very special to bring the best out of him. I realised that, as his chances of keeping his title became more and more remote, he would dig deep into his reserves of stamina and, just as he'd done against Benn and Watson, find the strength to pull off something special. Reminded by Ronnie Davies that he was just nine minutes away from losing his title, he stepped out of his corner at the beginning of the tenth and beckoned me forward. It was as though he were telling me: 'Come here, you young Irish upstart, and take what's coming to you.' We exchanged punches, but he took his time, set me up with a left and brought a thunderous right straight behind it, crashing into the side of my face. THUMP. The weight of the punch almost turned me around. I fell heavily, but managed to cushion my fall by grabbing one of the ropes with my left hand. Standing over me, Eubank thrust his arms in the air and looked down at me contemptuously. My brain was still fully engaged. Looking up at him, I smiled to let him know I was all right and, as the referee ushered him back towards a neutral corner and started the count, I nodded to Freddy in the corner to assure him that I was fine. I stayed down on one knee until the count reached nine, then stood up and told the referee: 'I'm all right.'

He waved us on and Eubank rushed forward. He threw a big punch as he charged in. But he appeared to be moving much more slowly than he actually was and, despite the knockdown, I still had the presence of mind to sidestep him by jumping to my right; he came crashing into the top rope and was left facing the crowd. He turned around and walked after me again, throwing two or three punches. My legs had been weakened, but I tried to kick some life back into them by circling him. He threw a few more punches, but my jab whipped back into life again.

Afterwards, people would suggest that Eubank had let me off the hook. But he didn't. We seemed to be alone in knowing that he couldn't hit me often enough to trouble me. Even after the knockdown, the round eventually started to assume the same pattern of most of those that went before it, with Eubank getting tagged by a couple of punches every time he tried to land one. He'd burnt up a lot of energy chasing me and he knew I'd fully recovered. Frustrated at his inability to press home his advantage, he stopped following me, stood at the centre of the ring and dropped his hands.

'Come on,' he said, trying to entice me into a brawl again. I jabbed at him. He dropped his hands again:

'Come on,' he said a second time, and I hit him again.

A right caught me plumb on the head and he kept his left jab in my face. Then he pointed to the floor in front of him, as though to say: 'I am the champion. Now, you come here and fight me like a man.'

He was appealing to some primal instinct in me that would cause me to abandon my tactics and fight him toe-to-toe. A knowing look and then a smile passed between us. Realising that I wasn't going to take up his challenge, he tried to embarrass me into leading. He stepped back against the ropes and performed a bit of a dance, before throwing a right to my body. He smiled and nodded at me.

'Yeh, come on, Steve,' he said.

'That was a good shot, Chris,' I told him. 'But you won't get me with another one.'

And he opened up his guard again, baring his chest and stomach to me, inviting me to come in. But, as I returned to my corner when the bell rang, my head had cleared and I knew that he'd enjoyed the best round he was going to have all night. He'd shown remarkable strength, resilience and character I didn't think him capable of by picking himself up off the floor to pull off this incredible effort. But I was more confident of victory than ever at the end of it.

Round Eleven: Whether Eubank knew that his chance had passed or whether he believed that the knockdown would be enough to turn the fight in his favour, he didn't have the same intensity about his work after that. A big, jarring right missed me by what must have been a foot and we were content to hide behind our jabs for the first minute of the round.

'Good shot, Chris,' I told him once more, when he caught me with a crisp one. 'But you won't do that again.'

He tried to get in under my punches, but got caught with two short, sharp lefts. Another reckless over-arm punch missed me and left him exposed on the ropes. I hammered him with both hands and, as I stepped backwards again, he was forced to take a good right. Seconds before the bell, he landed his best punch of the round, a good right. But it didn't justify another show of bravado as he returned to his corner.

Round Twelve: I sat down on the stool for the last time and filled my lungs with air, unaware until I watched the fight later on TV that across the ring Ronnie Davies was slapping Eubank in the face and shouting: 'If you don't knock him out or stop him, you've lost the fight.'

The pace had taken its toll on both of us. We were both pushing back the bounds of exhaustion as we walked towards the middle of the ring for the last time. After thirty-three minutes, we understood each other so intimately that we were probably alone in knowing that there wasn't going to be a knockdown. The referee stood between us, keeping us apart with his outstretched arms and he ordered us to touch gloves. The ritual over, Eubank charged straight for me in one last desperate throw. A barrage of wild shots missed me on the ropes and I walked away. His mouth was open and he was panting. The noise in the arena was intense and hearing the chants of 'Steve-oh' gave me the impetus to dig deep for the strength to stand toe-to-toe with him for the first time in the fight. We both let go with everything we had. I smiled at Eubank and he nodded at me, as though he respected me for withstanding what he'd just thrown. Onwards I continued, driving, driving, driving. Much of his work now had the mark of a desperate man about it, and he accidentally caught me with his head coming inside. He took the full brunt of it himself, stumbling back against the ropes and I punched him as he tried to tie my arms up. We exchanged good body punches.

With about a minute to go, I caught him with a solid right and he seemed to me to waver a bit. I looked down at his legs and they had buckled. Had it happened in the early part of the fight, I'd have finished him off. His hands were aloft again and he tried to taunt me. I stepped backwards and he charged at me until we fell back against the ropes, then, as he went to draw a punch back, I pawed at him and slipped away; and he fell against the ropes and was left looking out into the crowd again. Our arms punch-weary, almost to the point of limpness, we stood off each other for a few seconds. Eubank performed one last dance and beckoned me forward again. I threw an aimless shot in his direction and we fell into a clinch. The bell sounded.

My brother, Roddy, who has a remarkable talent for breaching security cordons and getting into boxing rings, was already standing in front of me by the time I turned around and started walking back to my corner. His two forefingers in the air in front of him, he looked at me and shouted:

'Means to an end, Stephen. Means to an end.'

It wasn't until a few days later that I realised what he meant.

THE NEW CHAMPION

As the audience erupted, I knew that I'd won the fight. Eubank had received the benefit of so many controversial decisions in the past, but nobody had beaten him as convincingly as I had. As far as I was concerned, he'd won the eighth by a 10-8 margin and taken a share in the twelfth, but I'd won all the rest. Whether the judges agreed with me or not, I knew in my mind that I'd won the fight and was entitled to feel jubilant about that. As we waited for final confirmation of the result, Eubank was having difficulty coming to terms with the fact that his luck had finally run out. Standing up on the bottom rope, he was facing the crowd and shouting: 'I've got a draw, I've got a draw.'

Their response was razor-shrarp. 'On your bike, on your bike, on your bike ...' they sang, as Freddy's son, Jason, undid my gloves for me and I walked over to each of the ring posts in turn, stood on the middle rope and applauded the crowd. Before I managed to get over to Eubank's corner, the emcee had the microphone in his hand: 'Ladies and gentlemen! We have a unanimous decision. Judge Roy Francis scores the contest 114 to 116, Judge Cesar Ramos scores the contest 111 to 115, and judge Ismael Fernandez scores the contest 113 to 114 for the winner, and the NEW –'

After that, I didn't hear anything else. I felt myself being hoisted into the air and somehow landed on someone's shoulders. I sat there, giving victory signs as I started to pick out faces I knew in this delirious crowd in front of me. Eventually, the belt was handed across and I held it aloft.

When the euphoria wore off, the exhaustion set in. The heat in the ring was unbearable and my habit of spitting the water out between rounds instead of consuming it had left me very dehydrated.

Ian Dark from Sky Sports was waiting outside the ring to interview me. New rules that had been brought in in Britain after the Michael Watson tragedy prohibited interviews taking place in the ring. But the crew seemed to forget for a moment that they weren't under British jurisdiction. 'Come on in, lads,' I said. 'You're in Ireland now. You can do the interview in here.'

Mel Christle was standing beside me. 'Yeh, he's right,' he said. 'It is allowed.'

So Ian climbed through. 'Well, here is the new champion, Steve Collins,' he said. 'Steve, what a night for you.'

'I had no doubts that I was going to win,' I said. 'Those who did doubt me, I forgive you. It's not your fault. Don't listen to the hype. Listen to the man, Steve Collins. I'm not just the best Irish boxer ever. I'm the best pound-for-pound fighter in the world.'

'Did you feel at the end of the fight that it was very close, especially after the knockdown in the tenth?'

'I had no doubt I'd win it. I haven't fought for ten months and look how easily I won tonight ...'

When the interview had been completed, we somehow managed to negotiate our way out of the ring and back to the dressing-room, where I lay down and poured what must have been a couple of litres of liquids into me. Then I asked for the oxygen. I could see from the startled look on people's faces that they thought I was going to spend my first night as super-middleweight champion of the world in Tralee general hospital. But I just wanted it to allow me to breathe more easily.

Then there was the press conference. I wanted to stress right from the start that I wouldn't be content to spend a couple of years making lucrative defences against second-rate opponents. I want to be remembered. In twenty or thirty years' time, I want people to tell their children: That Steve Collins was a class act. Fought and beat the best, he did. I've got my eye on a place in boxing's pantheon. It's right up there next to Marvin Hagler, Roberto Duran and Sugar Ray Leonard. And getting it, I explained to the media, means beating the best, like Nigel Benn and Roy Jones, who held titles of their own.

Very few people believed I could beat Eubank, which was reflected in the 3 to 1 odds against me winning that the bookmakers were giving a fortnight before the fight. Many people genuinely wanted me to win, but had somehow been fooled into believing that Eubank was indestructible. When I said in the days before the fight that I'd cover everyone's bets if I lost, most just considered it bravado. One man who didn't, though, was in my room with Tony Quinn and a few other friends when we got back to the Great Southern. Chatting away to someone, I noticed a man sitting on a chair in a corner, jealously holding this holdall bag to his chest.

'What have you got in the bag?' I asked, 'a load of money or something?'

'Yeh,' he said, unzipping it and showing it to me. Inside, in neat bundles of £10 and £20 notes, was £13,000 in cash that he'd intended to put on the fight, but couldn't lay it off when the local betting shops closed their books.

'Now, that's real faith.'

After spending about an hour and a half in my room with my wife, whom I hadn't seen for six weeks, and some friends, I went downstairs to the lobby, where a crowd of about two hundred people were waiting to see me. I stood on a table and signed autographs until my hand was sore and, after Freddy finally got me to sit still enough for five minutes to fix up my cut, I went to bed at about 4.30am.

Two hours later, I awoke. It was my first day as a double world champion, the man who finally undid Chris Eubank. But the only thing on my mind was the children, who were back in Dublin. It was seven weeks since I'd seen them. People wanted me to go to various places to meet people, but going back to the house in Castleknock to give Caoimhe, Stevie and Clodagh a big hug was the only official function on my mind. There were so many people to talk to that Sunday, so many dignitaries to be met, so many hands to be shaken, so many congratulations to be received, that it was 9.30pm before we finally thought about making the two-hundred-mile drive back to Dublin. But we decided the roads were too hazardous at that time of night and I might be another hazard, since I was so exhausted that I'd run the risk of falling asleep at the wheel. So we went to bed early and set off for home the next morning.

It was during the drive back to Dublin that I realised just how our lives were going to be irrevocably changed by what had happened that weekend. Feeling a bit of mid-morning peckishness as we reached Portlaoise, I suggested stopping off somewhere for a cup of tea and a sandwich. Gemma agreed and asked me to pull up next to a phone box so she could phone her sister, Niamh, who was babysitting the children. No sooner had she left the car than passers-by started to recognise me. First, one or two approached the car and asked for an autograph. By the time Gemma returned, they were swarming around me like bees around the proverbial honey-pot. This selfish feeling came over me that I didn't want to be here. I'd done nothing but sign autographs, pose for photographs, answer questions and shake hands for the past twenty-four hours. I just wanted to go back to being a family man. I was beginning to realise that that wasn't going to be easy.

'We can't go back to the house,' said Gemma.

'Why not?'

'Niamh said there is a group of about twenty journalists and photographers waiting outside.'

Another town, another phone box. This time, I called a friend of mine who drives a black taxi and explained my situation to him. I didn't have the energy to answer any more questions, couldn't summon up the strength to raise my fists and give another broad smile for any more photographs. He agreed to collect the children from the house and bring them to a secret rendezvous (which will remain secret, since I may need to use it again). 'Make sure you're not followed,' I told him, feeling suspiciously like a character from a spy movie.

Before the taxi arrived at the door of the house, Niamh told the children not to answer any questions they were asked on their way out. 'If they say to you: Where are you going? just say: I don't know.'

They remembered their lines as they climbed into the back of the taxi, which shot off down the road, pursued by a convoy of reporters' cars and an RTE van. The driver led them on a wild goose chase around the north inner city, past the Phoenix Park and around the Liberties before he eventually lost them in Arbour Hill and made his way to the meeting point. It was great to see the children again. But after a couple of hours, Aidan Cooney, my friend from 98FM and now my agent, managed to find me and told me that the evening newspaper deadlines were approaching. 'Okay,' I said, 'tell them all to meet me in the polo grounds in the Phoenix Park in ten minutes.'

I was surprised to find the journalists in good spirits when they arrived. They'd obviously enjoyed the cloak-and-dagger secrecy of it all, the exhilaration of the car chase around the city. This was what they became journalists for in the first place, wasn't it?

Anyway, they understood my reasons and when they went away content with their story we decided to check into the Burlington hotel again, since it was obvious that it was going to be difficult to get privacy at the house.

GONNA FLY NOW ...

Barry McGuigan had returned from London in 1985 with the world featherweight title and received the adulation of the people of Dublin while riding around Dublin city centre in an open-top bus. From the day I watched that, it became an ambition of mine to experience the same thing. Beating Chris Pyatt hadn't been considered big enough to earn me what I considered was the greatest accolade a city can give to one of its sports stars. And finally, I was told, I was going to receive it.

Winning the WBO middleweight title was, of course, as big an achievement as winning the WBO super-middleweight title. But this was different. Eubank was Eubank. People without even the remotest interest in boxing knew who he was. Many of those who watched his fights may have done so to see him lose, hoping that he would get his lip buttoned. An Irishman had done it. So it was very special and the people wanted to see me and to see the belt that Eubank had hung on to so tightly for so many years.

Wednesday was the best day of the year. Sunshine was a welcome sight as I whipped back the curtains in my hotel room and got dressed. The bus, I was told, was waiting for me in Parnell Square, but I wanted to go to Cabra first. The limo was waiting downstairs in the carpark and it took me off to meet Michael Fitzsimons, my friend from Dublin Garages. Because he'd supported me during the days when few Irish people knew who I was, I decided it was appropriate to begin the homecoming at his showrooms on the Cabra Road. He wound open the roof of a four-wheel-drive jeep and told me I could stick my head out through the top as we passed through Annamoe Terrace. There were hordes of people all over the road as we drove up slowly and I bent down to let them shake my hand and touch the belt.

There were throngs waiting in Parnell Square. As excited as a child, I clambered up the stairs of the bus and stood on the platform at the front; then we set off and turned right onto North Frederick Street and then onto O'Connell Street. Thousands lined the streets, as the bus slowly made its way towards the Mansion House, where, for the second time in a year, a civic reception was being held for me. People were taking up every available vantage point, hanging from every monument, from Jim Larkin at the top of O'Connell Street, to Daniel O'Connell himself close to the bridge. One group of children stands out so clearly in my mind. There were four of them. They couldn't have been older than ten or eleven and, given that it was a Wednesday afternoon, I can only presume that they must have mitched from school to come into town to see me. They first caught my eye as we passed the Ambassador Cinema, where all four of them stood on top of a telephone box.

'STEEEEVOOHH! STEEEEVOOHH!' they shouted. I waved back at them. Fifty yards down the road, as the bus drew closer to another telephone box, I noticed the same four lads standing on that one too.

'STEEEEVOOHH! STEEEEVOOHH!'

They were on the next one too. And the next one. And on every phonebox we passed along the route. As soon as the bus passed them by, they'd jump down, push through the crowds and clamber up onto the next one. And when the bus turned up Dawson Street, and there were no more phone booths to be stood on, they climbed up on lamp-posts. I remember thinking to myself that it would be brilliant if we could get the four of them up here in the bus with us. They'd gone to such lengths to support me.

Holding aloft that belt on the forty-five-minute journey between Parnell Street and the Lord Mayor's residence on Dawson Street was as excruciating as any training session I've been through. It must weigh 10lbs and, holding it out in front of me the entire way, I must have sweated my way down to the middleweight limit again.

When the bus turned into Dawson Street, I couldn't believe the sight. There must have been close to fifty thousand people there. There were swarms of them and I was led from the bus onto a huge stage that took up the entire width of the road. 'Gonna Fly' was an appropriate tune as I climbed up the steps to meet Dublin's city councillors. Looking at this huge throng of people, all cheering, all shouting my name, I was very emotional. It could be heard in my voice as I thanked all of the people who had kept believing in me and told them how that belief had helped me keep faith in myself. And I thanked the person who was my greatest inspiration, Gemma.

So much had happened in my life since I had last walked through the front door of the Mansion House. I'd been through so many experiences in the past twelve months, through sad and happy times, through so many extremes of emotions. It was only when I began to reflect on it that I realised what Roddy had meant when he said: 'Means to an end, Stephen. Means to an end.'

The past fifteen or sixteen months had been a microcosm of my entire life, with all of its joy and sorrow, its disappointments, surprises, broken promises, disillusion, elation, illness, laughter, tears. When I decided to become a professional boxer at the age of twenty-one, no anecdotes or words of warning could have prepared me for what I would go through during the next nine years. But now I realised for the first time that without all the upset and pain, I would never have gone on to beat Chris Eubank. I wouldn't have been the same person or the same boxer.

The death of my father when I was just seventeen; getting beaten by Sam Storey; losing two world title fights; the disappointment of my defeat in Italy; falling out with the Petronellis; suffering the depression of being an undercard fighter again; the arguments about money; the disappointments of Hong Kong and Boston – they had all strengthened me. I'd learned that experiences, whether good or bad, make you a more multi-faceted person. It was my past that had created the man who beat Chris Eubank.

So Roddy was right. Well, almost right. Back then, we all believed that all of the disappointments in my life had been gearing towards one big night. But once I'd climbed that summit, I noticed other peaks in front of me. So it was *exactly* a means to an end, because it doesn't end. I'd like to think there will be other nights in my life when I'll feel the same sense of happiness and fulfilment that I did in Millstreet. Whether I do or not, there are new challenges waiting for me, new horizons, new experiences, more joys, more disappointments, more happy times, more tears.

Tony Quinn put it rather more eloquently on one of the very first cassettes he gave to me. 'Life,' he said, 'isn't a destination. It's a journey.'

OTHER BOOKS FROM O'BRIEN PRESS

THE MAMMY

Brendan O'Carroll

It's 1967 and in the teeming streets of the Jarro, home of Dublin's dealers and dockers, Agnes Browne sturggles to raise seven children, the only legacy of her dead husband 'Redser'. With her pal Marion and an assortment of characters as colourful as the fruit on her Moore Street stall, she copes with propositions, puberty and the problem with Sr. Mary Magdalen.

And when she has time she dances with Cliff Richard.

£5.99 pb

THE GENERAL
Godfather of Crime

Paul Williams

In a twenty-year career marked by obsessive secrecy, brutality and meticulous planning, Cahill netted over £40 million. He was untouchable – until a bullet from an IRA hitman ended it all.

£5.99 pb

THE LONG WAR
The IRA and Sinn Féin,
from Armed Struggle to Peace Talks

Brendan O'Brien

The most up to date account of the modern IRA and Sinn Féin –
The secret route to the ceasefire; the Framework Document; IRA
– British contacts; The role of the USA; Hume – Adams initiative
etc.

£9.99 pb

TRAPPED BETWEEN TWO WORLDS
Experiences of a Ghost Buster

Sandra Ramdhanie

Parapsychologist, healer and psychic, Sandra Ramdhanie tells of
her extraordinary encounters with the supernatural– the haunt-
ings, strange presences and ghostly happenings which are part of
her everyday work. She advises on dream interpretation, developing your psychic abilities and self-healing. A fascinating book.

£5.99pb

IN STITCHES
The Diary of a Student Doctor

Dr John Fleetwood

A successful GP chronicles his extraordinary experiences and
adventures as a medical student in Ireland and the USA. He lifts
the veil on the mystique and gravitas of the medical profession.
Hilarious and horrifying.

£5.99 pb

ME JEWEL AND DARLIN DUBLIN

Eamonn MacThomáis

In November 1974, the first book to carry the imprint of the newly-founded O'Brien Press was ME JEWEL AND DARLIN DUBLIN, stories and recollections of Dublin and her people. It was a immediate success and has reprinted many times. This special anniversary edition is completely revised and updated by Eamonn MacThomáis. £7.99 pb

BIRD LIFE IN IRELAND

Don Conroy & Jim Wilson

A must for anyone interested in birds and birdwatching in Ireland. An illustrated guide to all the common birds of Ireland, with birdwatching hints, sites, projects etc. For young and old alike.

£6.99 pb

GREEN CARD BLUES

Shay Healy

New York City is a hard place to make a living, especially for an illeagal like Danny Toner. Playing music in the Irish bars is a drag, but on wya to get by. His friend, an undercover female cop, exposes him to some shady characters in the drugs underworld and suddenly it's his life and not his livelihood that is at stake.

£5.99 pb

AFTER THE WAKE

Brendan Behan

Collected stories, including previously unpublished material, by the renowned author of Borstal Boy, The Quare Fellow and The Hostage. After the Wake is an essential complement to Behan's master works. It is a delightful and entertaining windfall from one of Ireland's most loved writers.

£4.95 pb

ORDER FORM